M

Praise for Bill Littlefield's C

"'Voice' is a rare quality in wri
the presence of the writer on
selfhood. His *writer's* voice co
reading this collection a delig

—JACK BEATTY.
News Analyst f   ... *On Poi...*

"How wonderful to have that voice we love—all at once wry, brash and darn near profound—captured on the page and always at hand. Littlefield has an uncanny talent for seeing the mischief behind the obvious and for being right."

—ELINOR LIPMAN, author of *My Latest Grievance* and
The Inn at Lake Devine

"So a guy comes into the shop and says the driver's side seat in his Volvo is wobbly. We stick one of your books under the seat, bill him $400.00, and everybody's happy. You got any more books?"

—TOM and RAY MAGLIOZZI (aka Click and Clack),
National Public Radio's program *Car Talk*

Praise for Bill Littlefield's *Keepers: Radio Stories from Only a Game and Elsewhere*

"A rare experience. . . . A book that travels on many levels of fine writing . . . the history of a time—not just in sport—and an exploration of human nature." —W. C. HEINZ

Only a Game

BILL LITTLEFIELD

UNIVERSITY OF NEBRASKA PRESS   LINCOLN & LONDON

"Marathon Mom" originally appeared
in *Yankee*, April 1994.

"Bring It On" originally appeared in the
Boston Globe, March 28, 2004.

"War and Circuses" originally appeared
in *New Politics* 11, no. 1 (Summer 2006).

Manufactured in the
United States of America

∞

Library of Congress Cataloging-in-
Publication Data
Littlefield, Bill.
Only a game / Bill Littlefield.
p. cm.
ISBN 978-0-8032-6001-6 (pbk. : alk. paper)
1. Sports. I. Title.
GV704.L58 2007
796—dc22
2007004970

Set in ITC New Baskerville.

Contents

Acknowledgments

Thanks to everybody at WBUR and National Public Radio, where people have been supportive of my work since 1984. Mark Schramm and Anthony Brooks were my first editors at *Morning Edition*, where I was also assisted by Tom Goldman and John Ogulnik. Jane Christo was enthusiastic about *Only a Game* from the program's beginning in 1993, and Peter Fiedler and Paul LaCamera have continued to encourage us.

I'm grateful to David Greene, *Only a Game*'s first senior producer, and to Gary Waleik, who's been with the program since its beginning, and who has been our senior producer since 1997. No writer ever had a better friend or a more thoughtful editor. I've had the good fortune to collaborate with many other energetic, talented, and creative people who've made me feel lucky to be going to work each day. Katy Clark, Tess Vigeland, Jon Marston, John Perotti, Jennifer Loeb, and Gabe O'Connor have been among them, as has Karen Given, who has been an exceptionally valuable and versatile colleague. I'm grateful for that, and for all the work she did to get this manuscript into presentable shape. Thanks, also, to Amy Littlefield for her suggestions on the manuscript, which is better for her efforts.

Some of the commentaries in this book previously appeared in *Keepers: Radio Stories from "Only a Game" and Elsewhere*, published by Peninsula Press. I'm grateful to Don Davidson for inviting me to collect my work for that book.

Thanks to the publishers and my editors at The *Boston Globe Sunday Magazine, Yankee Magazine,* and *New Politics* for permission to reprint the stories that originally appeared in those publications. Thanks to Bill Heinz for reading and commenting on the *Globe* story, and to Marvin and Betty Mandell for inviting me to write for *New Politics*.

Thanks to Andrew Blauner, who interested the University of Nebraska Press in this collection, and to Rob Taylor at the press for his encouragement and support.

Introduction

Suppose you could be anyone, within the world of sports . . .
A superstar in any game, a person with all sorts
Of money coming in, not only just from what you do,
But from the shoes you wear and from the drink
   you're drinking, too . . .
And from the cars you drive and from the broker that you choose,
And from the clothes you wear and from the credit card you use . . .
But I digress. If you could star in any of our games,
Would you elect to do so? Look, I won't be naming names,
But people at the top of any game have problems, too . . .
They stand above the crowd and people know just what they do
Each time they leave their houses—"houses," plural, they have lots,
And all of them—those houses—are in preferential spots.
But if you have no privacy unless you fly your plane
To some secluded island that you own, well, that's insane.
So I would not be anyone who's so completely known
That he or she could not be sure to ever be alone.

Still, wouldn't it be fun to be so good at what you do
That when you do it, people gasp and shake their heads? It's true
That hitters, shooters, golfers, skaters when they are the best
Supply our need to know that somehow high above the rest

Of all that's mediocre, shabby, disappointing, flat . . .
Float wonders that can lift us past the dross of all of that.
So would you be a cause for gasping? Would you be a star?
Or are you, fin'ly, happier with being what you are?
It strikes me, as I ask the question, it's a silly thought . . .
But maybe few among the ones who lift us thus have sought
To be as large as they've become in our collective dreams.
They've all been working too hard to look up, perhaps. It seems
That stardom, when it comes, must have surprised at least a few
Of those who have attained it. Huh. I wonder if that's true?

Well, this one's gone astray, I guess, as musings often will,
Especially the ones that muse upon the living thrill
That athletes can embody when they triumph while we watch
Them making moments full of grace while doing things we'd botch,
And also on the cost that we demand those athletes pay
As they, in their brief moments, work at what we still call play.

Only a Game

1.

In the Name of Names, Because There's No Other Excuse

Justice Now

DECEMBER 20, 2002

I want Justice Now.

Or, more accurately, I want to have had Justice Now last Monday about 12:45 p.m., and I'm already through the tunnel into East Boston, which gives me time enough to get to Suffolk Downs to put all the money on Justice Now in the first.

At 86–1, Justice Now, running with a herd of forgettable $4,500 to $5,000 claimers, came from sixth, closed hard over the last few furlongs, and beat My Advantage by a head to pay $173.40 for $2.00.

Justice Now.

A whispered hint . . . a goofy notion . . . anything that nudges me out of my chair, away from the desk and the telephone and the word processor, anything that urges me out to the track that, on a cold Monday, one of the last mad shopping days, had to be nearly empty, serene in the strange way of an outdoor sport on an indoor day.

My friend, what a Christmas gift it would have been.

Justice Now.

The perfecta, Justice Now and the second horse, My Advantage, paid over $1,200. The trifecta was good for $27,201. But don't misunderstand me. I'm not greedy. I'd have settled for nothing more than Justice Now.

On some future morning I will open up the sports section. I'll idly glance at the thoroughbred charts to see what's running at the local oval, and there the news will be. I'll find the glowing possibility of . . . oh, I don't know . . . Fair Play. World Peace. Equal Rights. Right there in the small print I'll find War No More. Open Opportunity. Feed the Poor. Or maybe . . . Share the Wealth. Charity's Day. Nobody Hungry.

Or maybe not. Maybe Monday was my shot. I didn't interrupt my routine for Justice Now. Maybe I'd have missed 'em all. Free Food. Empty Shelters. Brave Struggle. Maybe, secure in a routine, I'll always miss them. I hope not. I'll try to be paying more attention next time.

In the Names of Boxing

DECEMBER 15, 2004

Favorites? How do you have a favorite? Designating a favorite would mean choosing between Frank Moran, who was billed as "the battling dentist," and George "Boer" Rodel, a handsome South African with a glass chin who earned the nickname "Diving Venus."

Some boxing nicknames are easy to explain. At the end of 1895, a Baltimore fighter named Joe Gans had managed to win thirty-one consecutive fights to establish himself at the top of the fisticuffs line. To the surprise of no one familiar with the way boxing promotion works, over the next decade or so there emerged Allentown Joe Gans, Baby Joe Gans, Cyclone Joe Gans, Dago Joe Gans (as well as the considerably more politically correct Italian Joe Gans), Michigan Joe Gans, Panama Joe Gans, and four different fighters calling themselves Young Joe Gans.

I learned all this foolishness from Geoffrey Ward's magnificent new book, *Unforgivable Blackness: The Rise and Fall of Jack Johnson,* and there is more silliness where all the young Joe Ganses come from.

Consider the fighter know as Kid Carter, whose real name was Edward Blazwick. He was, as Ward points out, "born in Austria to Croatian parents, but because of his yellow hair, he began his career as 'Young Olsen, the Gangling Swede.'"

Then there were Rough House Wilson, Truck Hannah, Bombo Chevelier, and Frenchy the Coal Man. And there was not only Battling Levinsky, but Battling Norfolk. Battling Norfolk? Any relation, I wonder, to the guy who fell beside Richard III at Bosworth Field? Battling Richmond might have been a better choice.

There is no lack of great and memorable names in baseball and basketball, of course, but only boxing gives us "Mysterious Billy Smith," who, according to Jack Dempsey's manager, Doc Kearns, was so named because he was always doing something mysterious, such as stepping on your foot and then biting your ear.

But a favorite? All right. A favorite. Reduced at the end of his career to fighting patsies, Jack Johnson once faced Blink McCloskey, whom Geoffrey Ward tells us was "so-named because before the bell rang, he carefully removed his glass eye and handed it to his corner man for safe keeping."

What's in a Name?

MARCH 20, 2004

Fans of obscure team nicknames and unusual mascots were left with mixed feelings after the first day of play in the men's NCAA tournament. The Salukis of Southern Illinois University were swamped by Alabama's Crimson Tide. (The fact that the Saluki, identified with ancient Egypt, is the oldest purebred in the dog kingdom, apparently did the basketball Salukis no particular good.)

On the other hand, the Jaspers prevailed. A Jasper is player for Manhattan, the team that upset Florida on Thursday. The nickname comes from a fellow named Brother Jasper, who introduced a number of sports to the institution when it was young, and also invented, perhaps inadvertently, the seventh-inning stretch, which spread from the campus of Manhattan to the Polo Grounds, and then to all the known baseball universe.

Anyway, the Jaspers live to fight and stretch again. They next play Wake Forest.

In the women's tournament, the fourteenth-seed team from the University of Wisconsin at Green Bay is prepared to rise from its almost certain defeat at the hands—or claws—of the Cougars of Houston. The Wisconsin–Green Bay team is nicknamed the Phoenix.

Campbell University, which last appeared in the NCAA tournament twelve years ago, fields teams known as the Fighting Camels. There are any number of schools with such mascots as Tigers, Lions, Bears . . . even Demons and Devils . . . but so far as I've been able to determine, only Campbell has Fighting Camels. Likewise, I think the University of California at Irvine has the only Fighting Anteaters. Inspired, I suppose, by the sound the anteater in the comic strip *B.C.* makes when his tongue finds lunch, Irvine's fans cheer by shouting "Zot!"

I've always been a sucker for any team nicknamed the Fighting Saints. That's what they call the men's teams at the college of St. Francis in Joliet, Illinois. The women's teams are, not surprisingly, the Lady Saints, though not, officially, the Fighting Lady Saints.

I rarely root for Duke, since the Blue Devils are usually a favorite, and I prefer underdogs, but if the competitors retained their original nickname, the Methodists, I might relent.

If I ever find myself attending a game involving a team from Mary Baldwin College, I will cheer for it. Mary Baldwin's athletes are known as the Fighting Squirrels.

Incidentally, while *Only a Game* analyst Charlie Pierce was peering over my shoulder at this commentary in progress, he told me that he once attended a game involving Penn High School in Mishawaka, Indiana. That might not seem immediately significant, but consider that the teams there were known as the Cavemen . . . and the Lady Cavemen.

Keeping the Book

JANUARY 17, 2004

Keeping the book at a basketball game means marking down each point scored so the guy running the clock and the scoreboard isn't entirely on his own. It also means keeping track of who's scored each point for each team, how many fouls each player and each team have accumulated (so the officials will know when to toss a player from the game and award foul shots, and then more foul shots), keeping track of how many timeouts each coach has called, and keeping track of which team gets possession after each jump ball so the other team can get possession after the next jump ball.

In short, keeping the book is a terrific way to miss the game.

So I always try to be deep in meaningful conversation when the coach of the team my daughter plays for looks balefully into the stands before a game and asks for a volunteer to keep the book. But last weekend he caught my eye, and I was it.

Keeping the book for this particular group is complicated by the composition of the sixteen-member team. At a given point, the coach may put out a lineup of Christi, Kristen, Krista, Christine, and Kerri, with Kiki, Kath, and Kelly kneeling by the scorer's table, waiting to come in.

There is no confusion with the fouls, which the officials always indicate by number, as in, "23, blue, in the act of shooting, two shots."

The problem comes when the coach turns to the guy

keeping the book, who, on Sunday, was me, and asks "how many on Christi?" unless what he's really asked is "how many on Kristen?" or "how many on Krista?" "or how many on Kristine?"

The other problem comes when one of the eight previously named players—Christi, Kristen, Krista, Kristine, Kerri, Kiki, Kath, or Kelly—scores while I'm still looking at the book, trying to figure for out whether the coach has asked about Christi, Kristin, or Krista, and whether any or all of them are in foul trouble.

"Who got that last one?" I ask the guy next to me . . . the guy running the clock and the scoreboard.

"Kristi," he replies, unless he's said Kristen or Krista, or Kristine . . . or even Kerri.

Though I'm pretty sure the final score's right in the book, Kerri or Kelly may have been shorted a point or two in favor of Christi or Kiki. Krista fouled out . . . unless it was Kristin. I'm not sure which one had five. It may have been Kristine.

I am sure that the next time the coach looks balefully into the bleachers for a volunteer to keep the book, he's going to have to find Kerri's dad, or maybe Krista's, or Kristin's or Kristine's, 'cause I'm gonna want to watch the game.

2.

Close to Home

Good Hands, Billy

5/5/2004

The directions to the school were bad. The only place to park was a tow zone. The first three doors we tried were locked.

It's like that sometimes when you're driving kids to basketball practice at a school you don't know in a town where the roads conspire to run one way the wrong way and somebody's been harvesting the street signs.

Anyway, my daughter, her friend, and I had just turned away from the third locked, metal door and started across the paved playground to try another when one of the kids on the far end of the macadam whacked a tennis ball in our direction. Hard.

"Hey!" the kid shouted. Maybe it was a warning. Maybe he just wanted us to see how well he'd hit the ball.

I bent at the waist—more easily than I had any right to do it—and scooped up the ball, which had come sizzling along the pavement. If I'd thought about it, I'd have flinched, and the ball would have rolled between my legs or kicked off my hand. But I didn't have time to think about it. I picked it cleanly off the pocked playground and tossed it back toward the game as if I'd been a shortstop.

There was a gratifying moment of surprised silence, and then two kids at once shouted, "Nice catch!"

"I used to have it," I said to my daughter and her friend.

It isn't true. But on some few days, I have had it, and flaw-lessly picking up that groundball and managing to toss it back into play without tearing my rotator cuff reminded me of another day nearly twenty years ago at Fenway Park. I'd been talking to Johnny Pesky in the Boston dugout. Eventually, he excused himself to climb out onto the field and hit ground-balls to some of the Red Sox infielders. I stood, watching, beside the batting cage, and by and by one of the throws on the way back to the veteran fungo hitter took a weird hop and bounced toward me. I flipped the microphone from my right hand to my left, caught the ball on a short hop, and tossed it back to Pesky.

Before he turned back to his work, Johnny Pesky smiled and said, "Good hands, Billy."

And now, thanks to nothing but a happy accident on an otherwise undistinguished evening, it had happened again. Again, I had good hands.

To paraphrase the words William Shakespeare provided to an aging magician about four hundred years ago, "that's the stuff that dreams are made on."

Soccer Granddad

11/4/1998

Both my daughters scored goals this past weekend, a first in the Littlefield soccer chronicle, and the older one enjoyed a bonus a couple of days later. She was trailing me when I picked up the dry cleaning on Monday . . . an errand I relish, since the place is run by John Papadopolis. He's a business-man, of course, white-haired, often tired around the eyes, but he's also: a soccer player, Major League Soccer season ticket holder, passionate soccer dad of a college player, soccer uncle of two more college players . . . the whole package.

"John," I told him, "Amy banged in a goal this weekend."

He dropped the laundry on the counter between two other piles of shirts and extended both hands toward Amy. "Ah," he said. "Was it a beautiful goal?"

Amy looked puzzled.

"Did the net billow?" he asked.

Amy smiled and shrugged. She has not mastered sports celebrity.

John reached under the counter and came up with a lollipop. Since my daughters were in strollers, he's been giving them lollipops. When they aren't with me, he gives them to me anyway. The glove compartment of my car is full of the lollipops I've neglected to pass on.

"Congratulations on your goal," John said solemnly. With a bow he presented the lollipop. Then he grinned. He is a world cup–class grinner. In the presence of his grin, you can only grin back or laugh out loud. Amy grinned and I laughed.

The bell on the door announced another customer, another man with an armload of shirts. John turned and addressed him. "This is a very lucky man," he said, indicating me. "He lives with three beautiful women."

As Amy and I walked back to the car, she said, "I can see why you like coming here. He's nice."

Amy's paternal grandfather, my dad, died when she was a couple of months old. When my wife's father died, Amy was only a little over three. She may remember singing for him, but I doubt it.

A long time ago a wise friend of mine told me that he thought we all had to find our fathers where we could. I like the idea that this seems to be true of grandfathers as well.

Alison's Game

9/1996

On a sunny September Sunday—a clearer, warmer afternoon than the morning had promised—a neighbor with a little girl who's seven, the same age as my younger daughter, called with an invitation: he had two extra tickets to the White Sox–Red Sox game. Would Alison and I like to go?

Alison said "Yes," and the neighbor and I agreed on the ground rules: we'd leave as soon as one of the girls got antsy, no matter what the inning, no matter what the score.

We needn't have worried. Alison and Erin, my neighbor's daughter, brought to the game enough stuff to entertain themselves through two rainouts—stickers, dolls, snacks. We could have set up shop in the grandstand.

The bonus was the game, at least if you weren't a fan of pitching. Even before we'd made our second trip to the restroom, Frank Thomas had hit two enormous homeruns for the White Sox on Tim Wakefield knuckleballs that didn't knuckle. Mo Vaughn had answered with one for Boston. Vaughn would hit another one. Thomas would hit three in his first three at bats, which set up one of the strangest dynamics I've ever seen in Fenway Park.

Though the Red Sox were behind and though the home team was still nursing a pale hope that it might make the postseason, the crowd cheered unapologetically for Thomas to whack number four. Those on hand opted for spectacle and a record over the ephemeral thrill of winning.

This was lost on Alison and Erin. When you bring stickers and doll shoes to a game, you drop them. Then you have to crawl around under your seat to find them. You can't see the ball field from under your seat. Still, Alison was paying sufficient attention to have noticed that the players on both teams were running around the bases continually, and when a multibase Red Sox error invited two more White Sox across the plate, she looked up, took in the circling runners, and asked, "Another homerun?"

"No," I told her. "The pitcher just threw the ball away."

"Oh," she said. And then, a little wide-eyed, asked, "Do they have another one?"

As it turned out, they did, and the game went on.

Alison and Erin watched for a while, asked again who was winning, and solemnly passed the score on to their dolls, who took the bad news well.

I tried not to smile. The Red Sox were losing. It had never mattered less. As it turned out, they would rally and win the next game, but that didn't turn out to matter much, either.

Next season, I will attend games with Alison more often.

Winter's Compensations

WINTER, 1994

If you don't think about how cold it's gonna get, there are things to look forward to in the winter in New England. This is even if you don't ski, and you live on a hill that's the last place the town plows.

Consider, for example, skating lessons for the kids. This winter, my kids will go together, fairly early Saturday morning. It will get them away from the TV. Even if no other good things happened, that would be sufficient cause to sign them up again and again.

But other good things do happen. My younger daughter, almost five, will try skating for the first time this season. I'm looking forward to it, because for the past two winters I've watched my older daughter get a little more comfortable and a little more confident on the ice each week.

That is not to say that there are any future Nancy Kerrigans or Brian Boitanos or Ray Bourques on the rink where Amy has been skating. In fact, there have always seemed to me to be more goofballs than anything else. The last thing that all the kids learn is how to stop, and many of them—especially the boys—seem to put it off intentionally, because they enjoy crashing themselves into the boards. The adults, wrapped around their paper coffee cups, cringe at each "thud." But the kids just laugh, struggle to their feet, and do it again. Nobody gets hurt. Helmets are required and everybody's bundled up. In their snowsuits, peering over scarves, the littlest skaters are about as agile as fireplugs, and about as fast.

But it is cold.

The lessons are in an outdoor rink with green canvas sides that buzz and snap in the wind, and sometimes the kids whine. Some parents exhort their children to be tough.

"Only ten minutes left in your lesson!" they shout. "Keep skating!"

Not me. Last year and the year before that, if my older daughter came painfully pumping and almost gliding her way out of the pack to tell me that her feet were frozen, I walked with her into the little, heated shed, helped her take off her skates, and rubbed her feet until she could feel her toes again. Then, if there was any lesson time left, she'd go back out and skate a little more. If not, we headed home. We listened to the acoustic music station on the car radio, sometimes singing along, and she'd ask what was for lunch.

This time around, I'll be taking both daughters. The littler one will gradually discover that she can stand on skates, and that she can glide a little, and eventually that she can chase her sister.

That much I know, but there's so much to discover. Maybe the two of them will push each other, and both will stay out on the ice through the whole, cold lesson. Maybe I'll be rubbing two sets of feet.

Probably on the way home one of them will scrape the sludge off her skates and hit the other one in the eye with it. Almost certainly they'll argue over who has to sit in the back, and maybe they won't want to listen to the same radio station.

But maybe, on some mornings, we'll all sing.

Gutter Balls

I had remembered bowling as a very forgiving game in which people don't get hurt and nothing much can go wrong. So on a recent, wet weekend afternoon, it seemed like a good idea to take the family out to the candlepin lanes.

Once there, things began to go wrong right away. In her very first frame, Alison, my younger daughter, knocked down two pins. They fell slowly—reluctantly—but they fell. This would have been fine, except that my older daughter, Amy, who is eight, bowled three gutter balls in her first frame and concluded that bowling was stupid.

By the third frame, I was ready to agree with her. That was when the younger daughter threw two balls that never made it to the end of the gutter. Each rolled for a while and then came gently to a stop, as if it had gotten tired or run out of fuel.

I had never seen this happen before, but I understood pretty much right away that I had two options. I could walk self-consciously down the alley, pick up the balls, and bring them back to the ball rack; or I could wind up and wing a ball down the gutter hard enough to knock the inert balls past the pins.

I chose to do the former, though I felt like a fool. With each step, I expected to hear the owner of the alleys shout, "Hey, you blockhead! What are you doing down by those pins!"

But he didn't, and nobody laughed.

When it was Alison's turn to bowl again, I told her to try to roll the ball a little bit harder. For a frame or two, she did, and though she didn't knock down any pins, all the balls made it to the end of the alley. This seemed to please her, and it certainly pleased me.

Meanwhile, my wife, who was scoring considerably better than both the kids, but had fallen behind me, began to needle.

"You're so competitive," she said. "Every time you throw

the ball, you get this look on your face like you want to break the pins into kindling."

"I'm just trying to knock them down," I said. "That's the point."

"The point is to have fun," she said. "Don't look so grim about it.

Maybe I was looking grim because of a premonition of what would happen next.

Returning from her seventh or eighth trip to the drinking fountain, Alison nudged a couple more balls about three-quarters of the way down the right hand gutter, where they quietly came to rest. This time I decided to knock them the rest of the way home.

I wound up, probably looking very grim, and fired a ball directly down the gutter. It was, unfortunately, careening side-to-side within the gutter when it hit the closer stalled ball, and although both of the balls Alison had thrown rolled obediently into the pit behind the pins, my shot bounced completely over our alley and crashed into the pins on the adjacent lane. That probably surprised the man who was bowling there. I'm not sure. I couldn't meet his eyes.

"Do those pins count on your score?" Amy asked.

"Absolutely," I said.

"No fair!" she said, and my wife told me again that I shouldn't throw the ball so hard.

By the time we'd reached the final frames, Alison was slithering like a snake around the molded plastic seat, and Amy had begun walking away from each shot without waiting to see where the ball went.

But, weirdly, when the game was over, they both wanted to bowl another string.

"No," I told them. "It's time to go. Maybe we'll come back another day."

And maybe, if I can ever forget almost everything that happened that day, we will.

Christmas Blessings

12/17/2003

There is a big, heavy tennis player, smiling as if she has just won at Wimbledon.

There is a tasteful little soccer ball.

There is a not-especially-tasteful racehorse, jockey included, that appears to have been formed from cookie dough. The horse is running across the word "Saratoga," making this one the only Christmas ornament I own that is actually sort of an ad.

These and several other sports-related baubles made their annual appearance earlier this week when my wife, my daughters, and I decorated our tree.

Missing was the glass Boston Red Sox ornament that had graced our tree for a decade or so. The Red Sox ornament wasn't missing because the Red Sox failed to get past the Yankees in the fall. The Red Sox always fail to get past the Yankees in the fall, except when they don't play well enough to earn the opportunity to get past the Yankees in the fall.

No, the Red Sox ornament is no more because last year after we got the whole tree decorated, sports ornaments and all, lights a'glittering . . . it fell over.

The crash was devastating. The children howled with delight at the spectacle. Colorful glass balls exploded into shards. A most counter-festive ornament, Mo, the bartender from the Simpsons, lost both his feet, and, oh, the humanity, the Red Sox ball was among the casualties. Never a fan of tempting fate, I did not replace it. May the Red Sox forgive me.

Anyway, apparently a new family tradition was born. When we'd finished decorating the tree this year, my younger daughter wondered out loud if the tree would fall down again. My older daughter said something to the effect that it wouldn't really seem like Christmas until it did. Remembering that I'd had to take all the stuff off the fallen tree, drag it outdoors, hack the trunk into a shape that would better suit the stand, then, with freezing hands, haul the tree back in so we could decorate it again, I suggested that somebody should maybe take the heavy tennis player off her perch and stand her beside the fireplace. Then I silently invoked the ghost of our crashing Christmas tree past to grant us a couple of weeks of humble, upright glowing and glittering. Not, I hope, in this season of blessings, too much to ask.

Aliens

FALL, 1995

This spring, I was an assistant coach with the Needham, Massachusetts, Aliens, a collection of nine-year-old girls that earned its nickname during the first practice when several of the young athletes picked up the orange cones we'd used to mark the sidelines and began running up and down the field with them on their heads. Aliens.

My chief contribution to the team was minimal: a midseason suggestion to the head coach and the other assistant that perhaps we should stop shouting contradictory instructions at the players, at least during games.

Probably for reasons other than that, the Aliens enjoyed a successful campaign. Everybody played each position, the team improved consistently, and the Aliens even won a postseason tournament and got trophies, which—as far as my daughter was concerned—was the highlight of her soccer career.

My own candidate for "highlight" came earlier in Amy's soccer days, though, on a day that she might not even remember. The previous year, 1994, as an even less experienced assistant coach, I watched her play for a team that didn't win any trophies. It was also a team on which none of the girls ever wanted to play goalie. The two circumstances may have been related.

Anyway, moments before one particular game, the coach designated one of Amy's teammates the starting goalie and pointed toward the goal she would be tending. The little girl burst into tears and ran in the opposite direction. These things happen among eight-year-old soccer players. With no prompting, Amy stepped forward and said, "I'll be goalie."

She didn't like playing goalie. She'd told me that. But to the relief of her coach and her teammates, she trotted out to the position so the game could begin.

At the half, Amy's team was up one. Still, nobody else wanted to play goalie. When the game ended—with Amy still in goal— they were down one.

As we walked to the car, I said, "I'm proud of you."

"We lost," she said.

"You played a good game," I said, "and you took the girl who was crying off the hook."

She shrugged. "Can I have a friend over?" she asked.

It is said that sports builds character. It may be true. But for this neophyte coach, this father who always seems to be saying to his daughter, "Enough with the smart mouth," or "Clean up your room," the more important function of that game was to provide a reminder that the character was already there.

Gifts

12/25/1999

On Christmas days at home—my home—sports and the paraphernalia of games have figured prominently. I can remember a Christmas when a New York Giants baseball warm-up jacket, orange on shiny black—outshone every other gift. Maybe my parents understood how great I thought that jacket was, but I doubt it. I don't think anybody but another nine-year-old boy could have understood. I wore it until half the letters had peeled off and the satiny material of the sleeves hung in shreds.

Many years later, on the day before another Christmas, my wife, who has no use for sports, led me to the enormous basement of a sporting goods store in her hometown in Pennsylvania. We were visiting her parents.

"Choose," she said, and while she and a salesman watched, I walked up and down the rows of shelves loaded with wooden baseball bats until I found one that felt right.

This was no empty gesture on Mary's part. One of the stories she tells of her childhood involves a closet out of which many baseball bats would invariably tumble with a great clatter each time she went looking for her coat. The bats belonged to her older brother, a teacher and poet who interrupted college to play one year of minor league ball and has been for years a very successful coach. Back then, he was just a gangly, pain-in-the-neck older brother who loaded the closet with a teepee of baseball bats on a hair trigger. For her to buy me a bat—it was a brave if temporary repudiation of her own stern dismay at everything baseball.

Neither of our children, daughters both, spring-loads the hall closet with baseball bats. They are, like their mother, blind to the charms of that game. Unlike their mother, they could play if they wanted to do it. That's the gift of time and Title IX. They don't crave the major league jacket as a totem, but neither do they resent the games as part of the restrictive world of men and boys.

Our younger daughter, ten, plays soccer and basketball with flair and energy, but to her the most important question at the start of each season is "how many of my best friends are on the team?"

The older daughter, several years into the process of the much-too-early winnowing that characterizes our town's too-serious soccer program shrugs off slights and low rankings. When I picked her up after the fall tryouts, I asked her how they'd gone.

"Okay," she said. "I had to go up against an eighth-grader

who was faster, and she beat me. But it doesn't matter which division I'm in. I'll be on a team. I'll have fun."

A friend of mine now involved in raising his second family said to me once of all our children, "They're smarter than we are." Probably that's as true when it comes to sports as when it comes to anything else. Just another gift—undeserved as grace—to celebrate this Christmas.

Overtime

12/25/1996

"Carefully pull the base apart into its two component halves."

This ran counter to my intuition, which is to leave things that are in one piece as they are. But I carefully pulled the base apart as instructed. It bent a little. It creaked. But it pulled apart. So far, so good, but that was only step one.

Santa Claus, having apparently recognized that he wouldn't be able to cover his whole route on Christmas Eve, had dropped one present off early at our house . . . a tabletop soccer game, assembly required.

The game features ten brightly colored, sturdy little plastic soccer players who slide up and down the base—the same one I pulled apart and would soon reassemble—and actually kick out a leg when you push a button at the end of the rod upon which the player stands.

"Slide the control rods of one team's A, B, C, and D players through their respective holes in the middle support."

I did this. I slid Player E into his slot, too, and you would have done the same. Then I snapped in four of the hole covers that secured rods A through D into place without incident, but hole cover 5, which was supposed to make snug the rod for Player E, didn't fit. I almost broke it trying to make it fit. Player E fell over. My wife told me if I broke the game I could count on taking it back to the store myself. On

Christmas Eve. I reminded her that Santa had brought it, and that he didn't accept returns.

If Player E had been functional, he would have kicked the plastic soccer ball at her head. I wondered if my daughters would accept the explanation that Player E on each team was injured, which was why they could only lie there and not slide or kick.

I looked back at the step in the directions which I'd skipped, as you would have when you saw how easily players A through D slid into their slots.

"Player E's control rod is different, because it has a connection slot."

I cursed Player E for his connection slot. No owner of a real franchise has ever cursed a flesh and blood player more sincerely. Player E, the stocky, pivoting show-off, grinned his Lucite grin at me. I popped off the four plastic clear clips, disassembled the two halves again, and realigned the wings of Player E's control rod so they'd move freely within his special, big-deal connection slot.

I did the same with Player E's opposing letter on the other side of the field, reassembled the two field halves, and found that all of the ten hole covers now fit just fine.

Moreover, the wings securing the goalies to their mounting pins snapped into place without breaking apart.

I leaned back and examined my work, and it was good. Players A through E and the goalies slid and kicked as they were designed to do, and it was just midnight. There are Christmas miracles, and there are Christmas miracles. This was mine.

Remembering Hedgehog

"I can't do it!" she shrieks.

My seven-year-old daughter, Alison, is sprawled halfway up a hill, halfway around a cross-country ski loop some idiot named "The Big Easy."

She turns her face into the wet snow. Her brand new skis are crossed, her mittens are soaked, and she wants to go back.

"Going back would take as long as going forward," I tell her, though I have no idea whether it's true. The map is hopeless. It doesn't show hills like the one on which we're stalled. But, I'm the dad, so I have to sound like I know what I'm doing.

"Get up over the center of your skis, stand up, and I'll help you up the hill."

"I hate this," Alison mutters. No seven-year-old should sound so weary.

Just before Christmas, cross-country skis for the whole family sounded like such a good idea. Now, on this brilliant day for skiing on this golf course in Maine groomed for the sport, Alison would sell her skis for kindling. No, she would pay someone to remove and bury them.

Amy, my older daughter, had mastered the sport in ten minutes. She is far ahead on the trail, occasionally looking back in derision, thinking of names to call her slipping, sprawling, younger sister. Oh, yes, one of the truly great family gift ideas.

Finally on her feet, Alison—with my hand on her back—is making minimal progress: a step forward, a slide back, a flailing pole, another half-step forward. We try pointing her ski tips out. We try side-stepping. Eventually, we make it to the top of the hill.

Alison sighs. "It's big, but it's not easy," she says.

I nod in agreement. We plug along.

By now, her mother and her sister are out of sight. Maybe

they are already making us lunch. This family adventure has become an adventure that has split our family in half.

Around the next bend we catch sight of the road. "Alison, if we cut over from here, I think we can walk home in just a few minutes."

She nods her tired, wet head. She would rather walk to Chicago than ski another hundred yards.

But on the next morning—gray, misty, unpromising—we luck out. Amy and I go for a quick glide on a trail called "Hedgehog." It's easier than "The Big Easy" and not as big. It weaves in and out of the quiet woods, crosses a brook, and looks everywhere like a postcard advertisement for cross-country skiing.

Amy suggests that we go back and get Mom and Alison. "She'd love this trail," Amy says. "No hills." My thoughtful daughter . . . my daughter, the altruist.

So, we return and collect Alison and Mom. And it works. Everyone loves "Hedgehog." Alison glides along like a champ. I even remember the camera, and at an especially scenic spot we encounter a solo skier who agrees to take a picture of the four of us: the skiing family, all four members together, smiling.

No one who gets our Christmas card next year need know it was ever otherwise.

3.

Just for the Fun of It

Giving Thanks for Contests

1/3/2004

We are a species given to contests. If there is one thing I've learned in ten years hosting *Only a Game*, it is that there is no activity that cannot be turned into a competition.

Consider belt-sander racing. The belt sander is a tool invented so that woodworkers can easily smooth planks. But inevitably, somebody decided that he wanted to have the fastest belt sander in town, in the state, in the country, in the world! The fastest belt sander in the world!

And so there came to be belt sander racing.

There is also wife-carrying. I can't remember why. Maybe simply because any number of men have carried their wives from burning buildings or other perilous situations, and some number of wives have likewise rescued their husbands. Perhaps husband-carrying has failed to catch on because women are too smart to attempt to sling their husbands over their shoulders unless compelled to do so by something more substantial than a cash prize.

Skillet-tossing is another competition we've encountered. Presumably it began when somebody noticed that some number of women had tossed cast iron skillets at some number of men. Happily, in the actual contest, the competitors toss their skillets at dummies dressed up to look like men . . . unless that's redundant.

Then there are various eating contests: hot dogs, hot peppers, chicken wings, and so on. The single most destructive contest of this kind is a competition held in Russia to see who can drink the most vodka. At a recent such event, the second, third, and fourth place finishers landed in the hospital. The winner died.

Just before the end of 2003, I learned of the first ever (so far as I know) fruitcake-eating contest. It occurred in Buffalo, New York. The winner, Sonya Thomas, a 105-pound woman, powered down nearly five pounds of fruitcake in ten minutes. She beat Eric Booker, who weighs 405 pounds, by a single bite of fruitcake. Thomas thus added the fruitcake-eating title to the chicken taco–eating and hardboiled egg–eating championships she already held. Booker will have to be content with the pea-eating and corned beef hash–eating titles that are currently his.

At the beginning of the New Year, I have a great deal for which to be thankful. Somewhere on the long list is the opportunity to marvel at so much stuff . . . from afar.

Sports for Fun?

10/29/2003

The tall, skinny kid with the child-sized shin guards that leave his shins almost completely unprotected had taken one step on the field when the coach, who was only sort of a coach, grabbed his shoulder.

"Who are you going in for?" she asked.

The skinny kid looked at the coach as if she was nuts.

"Just pick a name," the coach said.

"Robbie!" shouted the kid, as he entered the game.

Nobody came out. Maybe there was nobody named Robbie

on the field, or maybe Robbie knew that nobody was keeping track.

On the far side of the field, another player took a dive. He stayed down.

"Are you hurt?" shouted the coach.

The player raised himself up on one elbow and thought for a beat. "No," he said. "I'm just lying down."

These are high school kids in my town who really like playing soccer, but who didn't make the varsity soccer team. Or didn't care to try out. Or might have tried out if they didn't have after school jobs. Or if they hadn't forgotten. Or something.

They play on Saturday afternoon for fun. They shout encouragement to one another. They laugh at one another without malice. Some of them are fast and sure of themselves. Some of them are ridiculous. They seem perfectly happy to be running around together. Playing time is not an issue. They play until they need to stop to catch their breath. Sometimes somebody else goes in. Robbie still hasn't left the game, if he was ever in it.

"How much time is left?"

The question comes from the girl who's just foiled an attack by intercepting a pass with a nifty trap, then dribbling most of the way up the pitch, but then she lost the ball. Now she's leaning over with her hands on her knees, about twenty yards offside, should her team turn it around.

"How much time is left?"

"I started my watch late," says the ref. "About ten minutes, I guess. Play on."

The girl shrugs and runs on to meet the looping pass headed vaguely her way. There is no offside call. Nobody minds. Everybody's curious about what will happen next in this happy anomaly in the land of sports taken too seriously too early . . . this game played simply for the sake of playing the game.

Let 'Em Play

Bud Collins, the wise and funny tennis commentator, has said that you know the parents of teenaged tennis players have fouled up the works—and probably fouled up the players, as well—when Dad and Mom abandon their own work to manage the careers of their children.

It has happened a lot in tennis.

As far as I know, none of the parents of the little leaguers from Saugus, Massachusetts, has quit a job to devote him or herself to promoting Junior's climb toward the big leagues. I'd assume that's a good sign.

On the other hand, I did read something about a guy who'd left his business in the hands of others so that he could make the trip from Massachusetts to Williamsport, Pennsylvania, to watch his son play in the Little League World Series for as long as Saugus is in the tournament.

Who can say for certain whether the five-hour practices that characterized the preparation of the Saugus team are extreme for a twelve-year-old child? Probably only the twelve-year-old child, and if he's absorbed the all-American notion that the two most significant achievements for any citizen are, first, to be on television, and second, to win, then extremity won't come into his discussion of what he did on his summer vacation.

Last winter I visited briefly with Dewan Chandler. He played basketball for Boston College some years ago, though never quite as well as his schoolboy days indicated he might.

He was valuable enough that those running the basketball program made sure somebody wrote Dewan's papers and handed them in on time, enabling him to remain eligible, although not to get a degree. He was less than a star, which must have come as a surprise to him, because as a teenager he was celebrated as the greatest player in Boston. They had a day for him, Dewan Chandler Day, and he told me that in a frame somewhere there was a proclamation to that effect. He smiled when he told me about it. We were sitting in the hallway outside the gym at the YMCA. He was there a lot. There was no job to get in the way of his being there.

"It was crazy," he said. "I hadn't done anything."

That's a perspective no twelve-year-old can be expected to have found, especially when the professional broadcasters are favorably commenting on his patience at the plate, and, besides, the Saugus kids have done something. The achievement of reaching Williamsport and playing well there deserves attention. But the attention of a national television audience?

Maybe I'd see it differently if I had a child on the team, but when ESPN devotes glitzy graphics to twelve-year-olds, a little voice in my head says, "Just let 'em play."

Zebras

5/4/2005

Anybody who's ever tried officiating knows it's harder than it looks.

That's not to excuse officials in the NBA who miss fouls or invent violations during the current playoffs, but merely to suggest the difference between being a coach, player, or a fan, and being a referee.

Guys on the other team almost never advance the ball without traveling. Refs wrongfully assume guys on your team are traveling because they are unusually quick with their crossover dribbles and fakes, or because their feet twitch when they're clubbed from behind.

From personal experience, I can attest to how easy it is for an official to overlook these truths so evident to coaches, players, and fans.

My first experience as an official came thirty-four years ago, when I was asked by a colleague to don the stripped jersey of a linesman who hadn't shown up for a hockey game between two teams of ninth graders at the prep school where I was teaching.

I don't remember who won the game. I do remember two coaches, several parents, and a handful of fourteen- and fifteen-year-olds calling into question my eyesight, my skating ability, and my integrity.

Many years later, on another occasion when one of the real officials failed to appear, I handed over my coach's clipboard to one of the soccer parents on the sideline, stepped confidently on to the pitch, and, in a twinkling, forgot all the rules of soccer.

But the worst was still to come. Just a couple of winters ago, dragooned by an insane youth basketball league mandate that every coach and assistant coach had to officiate from time to time, I stood over a fallen girl who'd been mugged in the act of shooting. I awarded her two foul shots, because I hadn't noticed that the shot she'd taken while being mugged had gone in. The girl's coach and teammates were upset that her basket hadn't counted. The opposing coach and players were angry that she'd been given two shots. With a single call, I had alienated everybody in the building.

Now I am old with wandering—not to mention slipping and sliding—over rinks, pitches, and courts, and I can say that one of the few consolations of advancing age is that I will never, ever have to blow a whistle again.

Super Bowl XL

2/8/2006

A football game can end in roaring, cheering, crazy screams,
And it can end in players all fulfilling all their dreams,
And coaches celebrating that they never will be fired,
Until they are. But, anyway, the whole place can be wired

If that is how the game ends, say, on some last second pass
That someone catches in the endzone, sitting on his ass.

A football game can end in tears; there can be wicked pain,
If on the team that is ahead the quarterback's insane,
And with no more than seconds left, he doesn't take a knee,
But laterals the ball when any idiot could see
That if he'd simply held it, simply fallen to the sod,
He wouldn't ever after be considered such a clod.
A football game can end in tears at some bonehead mistake.
A player goofs. It happens, though it can be hard to take,
And no fan of a team so cursed will ever think it's funny,
Unless he has neglected to back up his team with money.

So cheering, sure, and tears, all right, it can go either way,
The games can break your heart. That is the price you have to pay,
But why can't the officials do the jobs they're paid to do . . .
Which brings us back to how games shouldn't end, because its true
That there is one result less satisfact'ry than the rest,
It gnaws upon the gut like some relentless, nasty pest,
For neither teams performing well, nor lucky, bouncing balls,
Can overcome the outrage caused by missed or messed up calls.
That touchdown was no touchdown, and that penalty appears
To only have occurred between the fathead linesman's ears.
And when the season ends like that, the biggest game of all,
That should have been the super one just ends up feeling small.

A clash between two teams of monstrous hulks and coaching men,
Who plot and plan while others sleep must never be again
The plaything not of fate but of a man who cannot make
A sensible decision . . . or a man who cannot take
The time to find an angle on the play he's 'sposed to see . . .
My gosh, I know they aren't paid much, but neither are they free.

So if there is one lesson that the Super Bowl has taught,
It is that the officials—although no one says they're bought

And paid for, should be competent, and each one on the ball,
Lest seasons end in arguments about a lousy call.

Ted vs. The Tumblers

8/18/2004

Ted Williams maintained steadfastly—and loudly—that the hardest single act in sports was hitting what a major league pitcher could throw. His reasoning has something to do with the challenge of hitting a round object squarely with a cylindrical club.

Partly because Ted Williams did not suffer disagreement gladly, and partly because a couple of generations of sportswriters celebrated him immoderately, a lot of people have embraced his assertion.

But what about turning a series of back flips on a balance beam, launching yourself into space so that the world spins around and beneath you, and then landing—boy-yoing—like a perpendicular jackknife on a springy mat as if gravity were not an issue, all the while smiling as if grace came easily? (Which, by the way, Ted rarely did.)

What about doing that while knowing that you'd get just one chance . . . that unlike the baseball player, whose trusty credo when he's goofed has always been "We'll get 'em tomorrow," you'll have no opportunity to make up for a missed step unless you can make the team again in four years?

Depending on your own favorite Olympic sport, you'll have your own remarkable achievements to celebrate: the extraordinary conditioning and endurance of the water polo players, the resilience of the swimmers, and beyond that, the equanimity of all the athletes in all the sports where everything depends on as little as few hundredths of a second, or, more maddeningly, what a judge has seen or failed to notice regarding how precisely a toe is pointed, or who has fouled whom and exactly where.

It is all so hard, and the great gift of the athletes is that they make so much of it look so natural, with the form their muscles have learned and the confidence they've achieved through grueling work.

I kind of wish I'd thought more about the marvelous, wide range of astonishing, all-but-undoable things athletes regularly do back when I was still playing ball, rather than just assuming Ted Williams, loud and confident, was right. It might have made hitting a baseball feel much easier.

What If They Win?

3/28/2004

It was the best of times, it was . . . Oh hell, it was the best of times. There has never been an off-season like it.

We got the best starting pitcher available. We got the best reliever available. We got a new manager, who arrived with the requisite optimism and was characterized by the afore-mentioned best available starter as impossible to dislike.

(Was ever a manager of any franchise anywhere set up so neatly? Terry Francona may be as likable as Curt Shilling says he is. He certainly has a pleasant smile, and during his job interviews, he apparently wowed Theo Epstein, Larry Lucchino, John W. Henry, and everybody else who either owns or works for the team. But Francona's winning percent-age during the four years in which he managed the Phillies was .440. Epstein et al. fired a manager who had presided over 188 wins in two years and cajoled the Red Sox to within five outs of the World Series. If the '04 Sox don't win the World Series, they will have failed. Failed. Failed. Failed. Amiability and a thorough familiarity with the glyphs of stats guru Bill James will count for nothing.)

Which is not to suggest that this marked-down bargain of a team (at least by Yankees owner George Steinbrenner's stan-dards) must fail for lack of management. It could fail because so many of the guys who hit well last season have been waking up at 4 a.m. all winter, certain in their bones that they will never hit that well again. It could fail because Pedro Martinez and Schilling combine to win forty-six games and none of the other pitchers wins as many as eight. Or it could fail because the Sox front office, mad as Midas for ever more revenue, insists on pushing ever more rows of preposterously expensive box seats in toward both base lines, until Major League Baseball finally orders the forfeit of all Boston home games because there's just flat out not enough room left to play.

Any or all of the above might be better than winning. Because though Boston fans say they want the Sox to reign as world champions and may even believe it, that outcome would likely bewilder rather than delight them. Were the Sox to win the World Series, it's cliché—easy to imagine the heartening spectacle of overturned and burning cars, the liberation of all the beer in Brighton, tear gas and arrests from Kenmore Square to Kennebunkport—developments of that nature. But doesn't it seem more likely that fans (as well as those who weren't aware that they were paying attention) would tremble in the scary novelty of this . . . this . . . winning, and that they'd wonder how they were supposed to make sense of the next day that would dawn—that day upon which they would have no new pain to embrace, nobody to blame?

Which reminds me: How, exactly, did Tim Wakefield escape Bucknerization after he gave up the home run that beat the Sox in October to Aaron Boone, a defensive replacement who understood so little about what it means to be a Yankee that he ignored his contract and played winter basketball, tore up his knee, and blew millions of dollars? This, of course, cleared the way for New York to acquire that shortstop/third baseman who was, briefly, the captain of the Texas Rangers.

But I digress. The idea here is to embrace the grand, unlikely spectacle that has constituted the hot-stove league just past and to understand the delights and damage of the last few months in the context of both the singular history of the little ball club that couldn't and the future it will build.

And so, again, this off-season was the best of times, especially for those of us who are fans of marvelous stories and who regard the local ball club as a blessing primarily because of its inexhaustible capacity to generate them. Because we also saw the Sox offer Manny Ramirez to any team willing to assume his contract (and fail to divest themselves of him), then attempt to acquire the best player in the game, and then watch helplessly as said player became a Yankee—a magnificently ironic development after Boston's front office had pursued Alex Rodriguez enthusiastically and publicly enough to insult the guy who's been the club's shortstop and franchise player for the past half-dozen years.

Like every Red Sox failure since the dawn of the dead-ball era, the botched deal was at once simple and marvelously complicated. And when that deal failed to go down, Sox general manager Theo Epstein quietly turned his attention to putting a competitive team on the field in April, secure in the knowledge that the acquisition of Schilling had already spurred a record burst in season-ticket sales. Would that the same could be said of his colleagues and coconspirators in The Greatest Deal Never Made. Red Sox CEO Larry Lucchino blasted the player's union as obstructionist. Fair enough. That's what management does. Owner John Henry went one leap further. "I'm not a labor lawyer," he told the *Boston Globe*, "but from my standpoint as an American, I have a hard time understanding the reasons for killing this deal."

While it may be difficult for a man paying his utility infielders millions of dollars for summer work to comprehend why the merry lads should need a union, to imply that their organization is un-American bespeaks an exquisitely uninformed view of U.S. (as in American) labor history in general as well as an ignorance of the rules prevailing during the first three-quarters of a century of Major League Baseball, wherein management's contempt for the players was thorough and, according to the owners' pals in Congress, right and proper as well. In his windy, winter contention, Henry sounded more like a contemporary of Charles Comiskey, the White Sox owner whose penuriousness helped provoke the 1919 Black Sox Scandal, than a twenty-first-century mogul who's already on his third team. Henry, like any number of U.S. presidents and CEOs, may not like unions, but to suggest that, as "an American," he can't understand the presence, necessity, and function of the Player's Association merely demonstrates what Steinbrenner has no trouble comprehending, namely that if you want a player badly enough, pay the going rate for the guy.

What other off-season has featured the denunciation of the Players Association and the blasting of the once and current shortstop's agent as a hypocrite by the Sox owner, the acquisition of players who may have the impact Schilling and Keith Foulke may have, the anticipation of the arrival of a quarter-billion-dollar infield asset, and then the grotesque surprise that came when the Sox learned that the man they'd been assured would be the captain and shortstop of the Texas Rangers would be playing third base for New York? We could almost be forgiven for failing to notice that over the weeks of baseball promises broken and surprises sprung, the Patriots enjoyed a pretty fair run.

None of this is to suggest that other Sox off-seasons haven't been studded with great expectations and greater stories. In October 1975, a Sox team rich primarily in promise very nearly snatched the World Series away from one of the most thoroughly stacked baseball aggregations of all time. When the Sox almost sent the Cincinnati Reds home second best, there was every reason to carry into that New England autumn the conviction that the young, confident, and thoroughly entertaining Sox would win a World Series in short order—especially because the Yankees had struggled through one of their two-manager years and finished an unpromising six games over .500.

But the following season Boston endured a two-manager summer of its own, and the team built around that promising nucleus (and the grim, albeit barren determination of Carl Yastrzemski) never got any closer to the series than the pitch Mike Torrez threw to Bucky Dent at the end of the end of '78. Then came the several years during which the aging nucleus got hurt, began grumbling, and earned the "25 players, 25 cabs" designation, until finally all of the fish jumped out of the bathtub, and eventually Bill Lee was traded for spite and ballast.

The winter following the 1986 season was good fun, too. Optimistic fans could conclude that the team that several times came within one unhittable strike of winning the series in the sixth game, and led in the seventh as well, would have a fair shot at success in the spring. But according to the estimable Peter Gammons, even before they began preparing for 1987 in Florida, the players were looking over their shoulders.

"[Bill] Buckner did point out that [Bob] Stanley wasn't covering first when [Mookie] Wilson's grounder went through his legs," Gammons wrote in *Sports Illustrated.* "For his part, Stanley took some off-season shots at [manager John] McNamara's decision-making process, and the pitcher's wife, Joan, was quoted as saying that Rich Gedman 'blew it' because he had failed to stop Stanley's inside pitch to Wilson. Roger Clemens, the Boston starter, publicly wondered why McNamara took him out of the game with a 3–2 lead after seven innings, and [Don] Baylor privately seethed at not being used. 'All season long we won as a team, and as soon as we lost, some of the guys started pointing fingers,' says Baylor."

At least some of the above sounds familiar. The '03 Sox made it to within five outs of qualifying for the series. This is a long way from winning it, as the '03 Yankees will acknowledge. Still, it was a fine ride with all the cowboying up and the lucky video and various other foolishness that hadn't surfaced at Fenway since the rally caps. The non-sports columnists, editors, and ombudsmen don't write about the game unless the stretch-run of the local lads has reminded them that Baseball Is Life and banished all concern for the ticket gouging that is unlawful as well as ticket gouging that is not. They all wrote about what a jolly lot the '03 Sox were and what a lift they'd given us in this uncertain time of alerts blinking from orange to yellow and back again like traffic signals.

But the plots of the stories here are never simple, so simultaneously we got Kevin Millar, the rally video star himself, waxing enthusiastically about Alex Rodriguez and thereby bruising the feelings of Nomar Garciaparra, who, we learned, had earlier characterized the Boston media as "evil." We got Garciaparra interrupting his honeymoon to phone the sports talk-radio guys and express his dismay that the Red Sox front office had romanced Rodriguez after Garciaparra had been not only dependably snatching up ground balls on owner-ship's behalf but had been comporting himself as an acceptable citizen as well, which, in the world of professional sports qualifies one for beatification, if not nomination to the Hall of Fame. Remarkably, we did not get Mia Hamm's reaction to her new husband's curious decision to make that phone call from their honeymoon suite, but that will come, no doubt, in time.

So will the answers to whether acquiring Schilling and Foulke will not only make up for the club's failure to acquire Alex Rodriguez but also carry Boston to a championship. Because it's the Red Sox, the certainty of folly and failure swims in the lane beside eternally springing hope, and who knows which of them will win by a touch? It's almost irresistible to answer, "Only those who have been paying attention." Schilling is thirty-seven and coming off a year when he got hurt and won eight games while losing nine. In Oakland, Foulke could pitch brilliantly, night after night, without drawing undue attention to himself. How many people would have noticed if he'd failed? The writers and fans in his new place of employment are notorious for noticing everything and making up stuff when there's nothing to notice. Ask Matt Young. Fair or not, the speculation that Foulke will never be comfortable enough to perform well here began before he'd even signed on, and the first time he blows consecutive saves, the rage and then resignation born of the certainty that we've been duped again will surprise and perhaps dismay him.

Or maybe he'll mutter a curse, spit in the dirt, and save the next dozen games he's given the opportunity to save. Maybe Schilling will turn out to be no further over the hill than was that guy Clemens when he was thirty-seven.

None of which would alter the twisted presence of Alex Rodriguez in New York.

They play the games so we can find out. But finding out, which is enough in some places, is not enough here. Here the finding out comes with stories—even myths—that would have no resonance elsewhere: the barkeep who shut off the TV and said in the dumb hush that followed the last out, "The sons of bitches killed our fathers, and now they're coming after us." That's said to have happened in Connecticut after the '78 playoff game against the Yankees, but it doesn't matter, does it? It could have happened in '67, or '75, or '86, or '03.

But communal myths and the inclination to take Boston losses personally notwithstanding, all Red Sox fans are not the same.

John Updike and Roger Angell are among the most accomplished writers of our time. They are Red Sox fans. Donald Hall's achievement as a poet is exceptional and enduring, and he is a Red Sox fan. One afternoon at his farmhouse in New Hampshire, Hall spoke with real agitation about how frustrating it had been to watch the Sox fritter away Game 6 in '86, not only because of what was actually happening but because the picture on his TV was so snowy that he couldn't be entirely sure that he was seeing what he was afraid he was seeing.

But the sodden clowns who rip their shirts off in April and October winds, paint their heaving, hairy bellies red and blue, spill beer onto their shoes, and regard "Yankees suck!" as all you know and all you need to know . . . well, they are Red Sox fans, too.

Do the sages and the chanters and all those who fall between them have anything in common? Perhaps only the conviction that they are special in their suffering. If the Red Sox don't win the World Series fairly soon, the team will not have won in the lifetime of anybody. People who root for such a team can, perhaps, lay claim to a kind of distinction. That may be what holds together what has only quite recently become known as Red Sox Nation, whether the citizens acknowledge it or not: not passion, not even suffering, but membership in a fraternity/sorority of loss wherein the only sure thing besides the loss itself is the mad, self-centered, but finally gratifying conviction that the failure is directed personally at each of them and that it will come with a story worthy of a long, long line of such stories.

One of the more recent begins, "What was Grady Little thinking?"

On one level the answer is simple: "I'm going to leave the best pitcher I've got right where he is, and he's going to pitch us to the World Series, and after we've won that, let's see those smiling liars figure out how to fire me."

Or less likely but more fun because more perverse: "I'll fix the front office for not expressing confidence in me. I'll leave this exhausted multimillionaire out here until his arm falls off, if that's what it takes, and they can whistle for their rings."

In fact, almost certainly Grady Little was thinking the same thing that Bob Stanley was thinking before it all came down around his ears in Game 6 of the 1986 series. "I was thinking how great it was going to be to be on the mound when we won," Stanley said with a shrug years later.

Stanley, of course, would merely join a long list of would-be heroes. In the 1948 playoffs, Sox pitcher Denny Galehouse never should have been allowed out of the clubhouse. Bill Lee shouldn't have tried to slip a second Epheus ball past Tony Perez. Mike Torrez should have taken Bucky Dent more seriously. Carl Yastrzemski should have waited for a better pitch. Calvin Schiraldi never should have been allowed out of the bullpen. Bill Buckner should have been in the dugout, watching Dave Stapleton field a routine ground ball. Roger Clemens should have been encouraged to grow up before he found work with the Yankees. Pedro Martinez should have told Grady Little he was tired. Jason Varitek should have told Grady Little Pedro Martinez was tired. Grady Little should have recognized that Pedro Martinez was tired. And, of course, if John Henry really wanted Alex Rodriguez, he should have been willing to pay for him.

But a couple of floors below the level where the cheap opinions circulate, down there with all the other convictions we ignore so we can get through the business and pleasure of the day, lurks the aforementioned truth about fans hereabouts: They're better off if the Red Sox don't win. Because each year some team wins. Some years lately it's the Florida Marlins, which pretty much proves that you don't always have to earn victory with patience and suffering. Other years it isn't, which proves that the distinction is fleeting, even if you do earn it. But the point is that the list of teams that have won the World Series within anybody's memory is long, and the list of teams that have failed to win the World Series because of circumstances so bizarre that nobody could have invented them is very, very short.

Boston fans are not rooting for a team that's cursed. They are rooting for a team that's blessed, if they'd only see it—a team better than any other at generating the sort of tales the ancients used to tell one another around flickering fires—not easy tales of annual triumph but long, episodic, sustaining stories of struggle, promise, and promise subverted, frailty, cowardice, terrible surprise, failure, and loss; in short, tales of each of us and all of us.

Can Schilling win? Can Foulke save? Will Garciaparra transcend the bruised ego or sulk like Achilles in his tent? Will fly balls landing around Manny inspire in him even less interest than they did last season, now that he's learned that the Yankees wouldn't take him for a lousy twenty grand? Will A-Rod hit .250 against the rest of the league and .700 against Boston?

These are intriguing spring questions. With luck, we'll see the answers to them take shape slowly, in complex, implausible patters, over the course of the summer meant for discovery. And if we're blessed again, the great delight for a fan of worthy stories will be delayed until autumn, when we'll learn, deliciously, how it'll happen this time.

Changed Utterly

3/2/2005

From Phoenix to Fort Myers we've begun to hear the crack
Of ash a'hammrin' horsehide and—god help me, let's go back . . .
I can't talk baseball that way now, although it is the season—
The old clichés won't serve us for a new and chilling reason:
Last fall, against the odds, against past history and fate,
The Boston Red Sox rose and smote the Yankees in four straight;
Not only that, the Sox went on to beat the Cards as well,
And what they did by doing that perhaps we still can't tell,
Except to say the Red Sox now are champs—a lofty perch,
From which the team, its fans, and those below must start to search
For reasons to continue with the hallowed rites of spring,
And with the grind of summer and with playing out the string,

Despite the absence of the plot that's carried us these years,
Through false hopes, wispy dreams, and, often, unrequited tears –
The Red Sox are no longer underdogs or woeful mutts
Their triumph in '04, like some great arctic breeze, just shuts
The door upon the fantasy that when the Bostons win
A new age fraught with happiness and glory must begin.

How can there be a season when the question doesn't stand?
When Boston's won already? What can save us from a bland,
Dull summer heavy with the feel of disappointment when,
If Boston wins in '05, they'll have only won again?

Don't get me wrong. I wouldn't change last fall's result a whit.
It's only that I wonder how this year we'll give a darn.
Now Boston is the champ, the coming spring blooms without reason . . .
I fail to understand why they should play the '05 season.

Fair Play

6/8/2005

I'll watch the ballgame if the center fielder mows my lawn,
And if the shortstop feeds my daughter's mouse when we are gone . . .
And maybe if the bullpen guys have time enough to do it,
They'd wash the picture window so that then we can see through it.

I'll care about the draft the NBA's about to run
If two or three tall guys can clean our gutters. When they're done,
They might wash off the ceiling in the shower. What the heck?
Each time I do it, man, I wake up with the stiffest neck
I've ever had since last I did the job, and who needs those?
Meanwhile, I'll go see hockey if the whistle ever blows,
When several Rangers and a Maple Leaf or L.A. King
Come over with a tamper and some cold pack. Here's the thing . . .
My driveway's got these holes. They're getting bigger all the time.
A wheel goes in, I might not get back out, so where's the crime
In asking if some hockey players might put in some patches?

And while they're on the job, there are some small but ugly scratches
Across the Camry's door. A little touch-up paint, we're good.

Now you may feel I'm out of bounds, and that I never should
Expect more from the players than they're all paid to provide:
Exciting entertainment and a great, unscripted ride
From starting pitch to final out or long, last-second shot,
And most times I agree that's all there is and they are not
Obliged to earn my loyalty by any other means,

But lately life's been crowding in, so if the sticky screens
That prob'ly need replacing could be dealt with by an end
Or quarterback or safety, then those guys would have a friend
In me. I'd buy a ticket, paint my face, and scream and cheer,
But otherwise with all the chores I've got I can't go near
A stadium or even a TV when games are going.
In fact, at times when normally the tube would be a'glowing
With baseball or with basketball or football or such stuff,
I might be doing laundry, which, is not exactly tough:
A tennis pro could do it, or a golfer, it's a cinch.
The guys who drive in NASCAR could all manage in a pinch.
I know the athletes are supposed to have me all inspired,
But, heck, sometimes by Saturday, these jobs have got me tired,
And though the athlete's mission is to bear my childlike dreams,
Right now I'd take some less dramatic "bearing." If that seems
Irrational and silly, well, I've no time to debate.
I said I'd pick the kids up, and I think I'm running late.

Mind Games

7/2/2005

All right. A confession. Or, at least an acknowledgement.

I was a play-by-play kid. This was long before the advent of take-home-a-shiny-CD-of-your-own-performance-at-the-ball-park days.

My play-by-play experience came in the shadow of the garage in the driveway behind the house where I grew up in New Jersey. The key features of the garage were a door, a shingle roof, and, most significantly, a gutter that ran the length of that roof. When I stood at the edge of the driveway and threw a tennis ball against the door, it came back as a grounder. When I threw it against the roof, it came back as a fly. But when I could hit the curved lip of the gutter just right, the ball would take off on a line and soar over my head, over the curb behind me, even over the flower bed and into the crabgrass of our narrow backyard.

For hour after hour during the summers of my childhood, the Giants would play hapless opponents on that driveway . . . "hapless" because the Giants, who moved from New York to San Francisco when I was eight, always won. Opposing pitchers were especially hapless when Willie Mays came to the plate, because his grounders off the door and flys off the roof were almost always foul balls . . . prelude to when I could hit the gutter just right and create a homerun for my favorite player.

"Mays has fouled off another one . . . this one into the seats behind third base. Spahn wipes his brow. It's August-hot at the Polo Grounds today, fans, and he may be getting tired. And here's the next pitch . . . Mays hits it deep to center field . . . Warren Spahn has turned to watch this one go . . . and it's four to nothing Giants, as Don Mueller, Whitey Lockman, and Alvin Dark cross the plate in front of Willie Mays!"

I don't know who lives in that house in New Jersey now. Maybe if the family there has kids, one of them has already been to the ballpark in Philadelphia and made a CD of himself calling half an inning of a real major league game. But I like to think that the driveway and the garage with the door, the roof, and the gutter are still intact, just in case on some hot day this summer when the cable's out, the video games are broken, and everybody else is at soccer camp, that kid figures out that with a tennis ball and some imagination, he can create a game of his own.

All Stars

7/13/2003

There should be all-star architects, and all-star plumbers, too . . .
The latter could all gather to clear pipes clogged up with goo,
As thousands cheered the water as it whooshed down pristine drains.
There should be all-star astronauts, and researchers with brains
More active than the brains of those who work in other labs
Should also be named all-stars, even if their pecs and abs
Don't bulge. All-star mechanics should be honored for their touch
With cranky engines, and for never charging us so much
That we must dig into our savings to reclaim our cars . . .
There should be all-star waiters too, and folks who work in bars
Should also be called all-stars if they're pleasant and discreet,
And shouldn't maids be all-stars if the rooms they clean are neat?
There should be all-star singers, those who never miss a note,
And sing with spontaneity, and not as if by rote.
And all-star painters wouldn't see themselves as in a rut;
They'd never spatter paint around or paint the windows shut.
When I'm in a convenience store, and I'm served by a jerk
Who's stoned or lost in space, I wish I had an all-star clerk . . .
A man or woman, boy or girl, who doesn't snarl or bite,
And can provide directions if I'm lost, alone, at night,
And not just shrug and tell me that he doesn't know the way
To any place I'm going so just hurry up and pay.
There should be all-star help desk folks, who, though they know it all,
Don't make the rest of us feel dumb each time we have to call.
There should be all-star cleaners, who would never lose our stuff,
And all-star blackjack dealers would say, "Pal, you've lost enough,"
And point us toward the door before we pawned our shirt and shoes.
The all-star games for athletes always make the TV news . . .
But why should they have all the fun and all the glory, too?
There should be all-star everythings. No matter what you do,
You should be on the ballot, though I don't know who would vote,
And as an all-star, when you won, I'm sure you wouldn't gloat.

The Better Game

11/9/2005

The World Series concludes an overlong season and is often played in weather in which pitchers can't feel the ball and batters secretly hope they'll miss, since making contact with the ball will hurt.

Major League Soccer's championship is played in weather perfect for soccer.

Both teams that play in the Super Bowl feature dozens of bloated men who, by virtue of the size they've achieved to secure their jobs, run an absurdly high risk of dying young.

Both teams in the Major League Soccer championship game are made up of superbly conditioned athletes who can run all day.

David Stern, the Commissioner of the National Basketball Association, says one of his league's most splendid achievements is that it has become international. The NBA's players hail not only from the U.S., but from Congo, China, Brazil, and Italy, to name just a few.

Major League Soccer's players have come from an even wider variety of places, because they don't have to be nine feet tall to make a roster.

Parking at National Football League games is an experience that sensible fans will not endure sober. Only a fool tries getting out of the parking lot after an NFL game without a weapon.

Parking at Major League Soccer games is easier than parking at most shopping malls . . . on Sunday night.

Fans at Major League Baseball games have been known to run on to the field and assault umpires. Crowds at National Basketball Association games have been known to engage in hand to hand combat with the aforementioned nine-foot-tall players. Paying customers at NFL games—those sufficiently ambulatory to make it from the parking lot to the game— have been known to wear canine masks and howl at a moon only they can see.

Crowds—to use that term in its loosest possible form—at Major League Soccer games are made up of cheerful families; young, uniformed players accompanied by their dedicated coaches; and hyphenated Americans homesick for the beautiful game they've left behind and so grateful for soccer's presence here that it would never occur to them to misbehave.

On the eve of Major League Soccer's tenth championship game, the ignorant and the philistine still ask whether the world game has arrived. The rest of us understand that it has prevailed.

Racing Days

8/10/2005

In winter, working's easy. I just sit here at my screen
And type in what needs typing. Ah, you know the stuff I mean.
It might be hard to get to work, the driving might be tough,
But once I'm here, it's warm and bright, and that's about enough
To banish the distractions that might otherwise intrude
Upon the work of scribbling 'bout our games, and I'm imbued
With concentration that's sufficient. Outside is a mess:
The cars slide into snow banks on the street below, so guess
Where I would rather be? Stuck in the weather or right here,
Just typing what needs typing. You can see the choice is clear.

But come the month of August, working's quite another thing,
For as I type, I know a little west of here the king
Of sports—or sport of kings—whichever, is transpiring daily
At Saratoga. Horses run, and all of them would pay me
If only I were there instead of here. I'm sure it's true . . .
I'd breakfast on fresh strawberries, and that's not all I'd do.
I'd sip hot coffee at the rail and figure all the races.
I'd pick not only winners but the shows as well, and places.
But first I'd watch the morning works, and read and mark
    the form . . .
And marvel at the lawns of green, and clear air from the storm

That washed away the heat that sometimes burdens trackside days.
They would be cool, those mornings, were I there, and all the bays
And grays and browns and blacks all set to win would see me there,
And wink, and I would never miss the signals, and with care
But joyfully I'd make my bets, and when the day was done,
I'd wander into town and celebrate with what I'd won . . .
But celebrate with class and moderation, since the knack
Of picking winners means I'd have my breakfast at the track.
While losers still were sleeping, I would learn what losers missed,
Because they hadn't seen the horses pound out of the mist,
Before the sun dispersed it and the crowd filled up the place . . .
I'd find myself in tune with that sweet track, that magic place.

Or so I like to think. It is the vision that I choose . . .
And if I don't attend the races, well, I never lose.

Lance Un-retired

9/7/2005

For Lance six weeks of beer and kids has been, I guess, enough.
He learned that kicking back and watching children can be tough
Compared to riding like a fiend for hours every day . . .
And so he's un-retired and he will make the Frenchmen pay
For every nasty thing they've said about each doping test
They're claiming that he failed. He said this week "this is the best"
Of all the ways that I could find to irritate the French,
And so I'm back in training and no longer on the bench.

Meanwhile, in San Francisco, Barry Bonds was back in play . . .
Or if he wasn't, he was somewhat closer every day,
And he was telling writers that he knew he still could hit,
And not, as he had been before, suggesting they eat . . . uh,
    their words.
And when they asked if coming back meant he would play full time,
He made a joke about his age and laughed, a sound sublime
In what had been a story of suspicion, lies, and blame . . .
So Barry, just like Lance, is back to play, again, his game.

Meanwhile, the falling Orioles shipped out their damaged hitter,
But Rafael Palmeiro says that he's no more a quitter
Than Lance has been or Barry is, so Rafe's coming back,
Despite the ridicule of fans who mounted an attack
So loud that he wore earplugs when he sauntered to the plate,
While two for twenty-six with just one RBI of late.

So what's the moral of this week's regenerated crew?
I guess old athletes much prefer the doing what they do
To hanging up their gloves and bats and taking off their spikes,
Or casting off their helmets and relinquishing their bikes
For days bereft of adulation, even if that comes
With leather-lunged contentions that the lot of them are bums
And cheaters, dopers, disappointments, gods with feet of clay
Who'd serve the public better if they'd simply go away.

It's hard, I guess, to leave the spotlight when you need to prove
The French are wrong or you are clean or you can find the groove
That will provide another shot of glory and acclaim,
A drug perhaps as strong as any anyone can name.

Younger and Younger

10/5/2005

The stiff neck that I wake with and the pain behind my knee
Are earned. I am a beat-up guy, as any guy might be
Who's worked and raised up kids and also played a little sports . . .
And I could live with all the dings, but for this week's reports
That seem to me to make a case that time is not the stuff
That qualifies a person in the world of sports. It's tough,
In any case, to see the stars get younger every day,
But when the GM's do it too, what's left for us to say?

The Rangers, in a bid to move from merely blah to great,
Have hired a general manager who's only twenty-eight.
I guess this would be well and good, acceptable and fine—
Two years ago the Red Sox guy was only twenty-nine—
But in the week the news in Texas broke we came to know

That golf's most stunning prodigy is really turning pro,
And when the news of that appeared on my computer screen,
Michelle Wie, who's the prodigy, was not yet quite sixteen.

Not quite sixteen. The context to which you'll, perhaps, relate
Is that Ms. Wie, in years, has not yet quite reached two times eight.
Her peers are dreaming of a day that's still some time away
When they can drive to school. Meanwhile, Michelle will weekly play
With women who hire baby-sitters older than Michelle . . .
And cannot hit the ball as far or hit it half as well
As she can. It's some solace that Ms Wie will hike the pay
Of all the women on the tour, as Tiger in his day,
Did for the men, who didn't much resent the way he won
The biggest prizes on the tour when he had just begun . . .
But what of all the baseball men who've worked for years as scouts
Or personnel directors because owners had their doubts
If they were truly ready to make trades and build a team,
When they were not yet fifty-five or sixty? Might it seem
A terrible injustice to these patient, solid, sad
Guys, when a fellow far too young to be Michelle Wie's dad
Achieves the top job with the Rangers. Gee, he's twenty-eight.
Don't get me wrong. I wish him luck. I hope it turns out great . . .
But if these trends continue, golfers will know it's too late
To play the game at all if they can't play it when they're ten,
And guys who work in offices will have to think again
Before deciding sixty five's a happy quitting time;
At sixty-five they'll be about four decades past their prime.

Mannyland

12/21/2005

Among other items, there were several pairs of Manny's shoes.

"Yeah," one of the guys who works at the Boston area memorabilia shop called Sportsworld told me, "those cleats are really jumping off the shelf."An irresistible image, and not the only one.

According to Phil Castinetti, who owns Sportsworld, the most remarkable impression associated with his acquisition of much of the professional wardrobe of Red Sox outfielder Manny Ramirez involved the sheer bulk of the haul, which was apparent as soon as he entered Ramirez's home last October.

"When I walked up there," he told me, "there was stuff all over the place . . . the living room, the bedroom, everywhere."

None of the stuff was hot, at least according to the connotations normally associated with the word, but you wouldn't have known that from the way his conversation with Mr. Ramirez began, according to Mr. Castinetti.

"I asked him, 'What do you want to do here?'" he told me.

"I want to do something," said Manny.

What? Was each of them afraid the other was wearing a wire?

Eventually they did something. Manny found a pen somewhere under one of his investments and signed everything. Mr. Castinetti left the premises with twenty-four game-worn autographed Manny Ramirez jerseys, the aforementioned shoes, and lots of other stuff. Mr. Ramirez waved goodbye with the hand that wasn't occupied with a paper sack full of cash.

"Twenty-four jerseys?" I asked. "How'd he get hold of twenty-four jerseys?"

"They're allowed so many a year," Phil Castinetti said, "and then they can buy more."

"So these guys are buying extra jerseys so they can sell them? Even though they're making twenty million dollars a year?"

"From what I understand, Manny's very tight with a buck," said Phil Castinetti. "But, hey, at the end, Pete Rose was doing like a jersey an inning. When he won his three hundredth game, Gaylord Perry changed jerseys every inning."

Mr. Castinetti probably could have told me more stories

about who'd worn how many of what and then sold them, but
he didn't have time. He had to get back to selling cleats and
jerseys and everything else he'd hauled out of Manny's place.

"It's crazy here," he told me.

I'll say.

No Bracket Guy

3/15/2006

I'd eagerly embrace the madness
March is made of, but the sadness
Has, instead, o'rwhelmed us all;
Our bracket guy has heard the call
Of working elsewhere. What a mess!
We weep, we moan, we're bracket-less.

In other Marches—happy days—
We made our picks, wrote down our plays
And gave them all to bracket guy,
Who organized them, neat as pie,
And told me as the teams played on
In March's brilliant marathon
How I was doing vis-à-vis
The other bettors. Sorry, see,
I didn't mean it. Bettors? No,
We all were playing only, so
The bracket-building was in fun
Unless, of course, you went and won,
In which case, bracket guy would line
Your pockets. Nah, he would confine
Himself to saying "Congratulations!"

Maybe at the other stations
And in other working places
People still have happy faces,
Since, as March's days go by,
They'll hear from their bracket guy.

"What are your picks?" he'll smile and ask.
"Forget that loathsome, boring task
That might have had you working late.
It's bracket time! Can NC State
Beat California? Will Pacific
Upset BC?" It's terrific
When the place you work each day
Is transformed to a place of play,
And better, still, when you can make
A lot of money if you take
A longshot on the upswing. Ooops.
Did I say money? Nah, in hoops
As played in March it's just the thrill
Of guessing right. I promise. Still,
You cannot guess or pick or try
To win without a bracket guy,
And that's the rut we're in today.
While elsewhere grinning workers play,

And moan about how, having not
Foreseen that Bucknell would get hot,
They went with Arkansas and so
Their brackets are a shambles. Oh,
Can ever March be mad again?
I doubt it, as I chew my pen
And bite my lip so I won't cry . . .
For here there is no bracket guy.

Incredible

6/21/2006

"Did you see that game yesterday?"

I heard the question bouncing loudly off the shower room walls as I sat in front of my locker, pulling on one of my socks.

It was not a surprising question. The men—young and old—who stop at the gym on their way to work often talk sports.

"Incredible," came the answer.

"Incredible?" I wondered. "Incredible that the Red Sox beat the Washington Nationals?" Because my first guess was that the question referred to the previous evening's baseball game, which the Sox had won, 11–3. Decisive, but not incredible.

But maybe the guy in the shower room meant Game 6 of the NBA finals, in which the Miami Heat completed a comeback from being down two games to none to beat the Dallas Mavericks and win the championship . . . a result that was at least somewhat surprising, although for a team featuring Dwayne Wade and Shaquille O'Neal, not really "incredible," either.

"Yeah, that goal in the ninetieth minute," said the first guy.

"That," the second guy said, "and England lost Michael Owen in the first minute with the knee. You think he comes back in the next round?"

These guys, both of whom certainly sounded as if they were citizens of the United States, were talking about Tuesday's soccer game between England and Sweden. They were talking about a game in which the U.S. didn't figure. They were talking about a draw.

"Incredible," I thought.

I am careful about drawing conclusions from anecdotal evidence, but I make exceptions when the anecdotes support conclusions that delight me. Based on the conversation I overheard at the gym on Wednesday morning, interest in soccer in general and the World Cup in particular is skyrocketing in this previously sports-backward nation. Can an appreciation for ethnic diversity and styles other than our own be far behind? Next we'll all recognize that "World Series" is a pompous, fraudulent characterization of the baseball championship of North America.

My hopes rise like a ball chipped deftly over the keeper's out-
stretched fingers, into the top, right-hand corner of the net.
Incredible.

No Soccer Today?

6/28/2006

For nineteen days there were three games, except when there were
two.
Today I'm told that there are none. What is a fan to do?
I could go surfing through the channels, hoping I might find
A game that's somehow happening. It is, I think, unkind
To cut a man off cold when he's accustomed to the sight
Of soccer all day long and of the wrap-up ev'ry night.

Perhaps two teams who've not gone through will meet upon some
pitch
Where no one needs to practice, and, if only I can switch
The channels very rapidly I'll find the magic place
Where soccer is still happening. How else can I replace
The happy wave of game on game that's been my daily fare?
What is a lad to do when soccer's suddenly not there?

I don't pretend it's all been great. There have been brutal games,
And calls beyond belief, although I won't go naming names,
Except to say that Italy must thank its lucky star
That they received the call that put them where they bloody are . . .
But I would watch an ugly game, with refs who couldn't see,
A game besmirched with fouls, I guess, a game that couldn't be
Much worse if it were played in mud or in a sea of sand
I'd settle for game that could be tedious or bland . . .
But now, to have no games at all? No matter where I look?
I am, I fear, a victim, lost, as if a subtle crook
Had crept into the world I know and stolen all the joy
That has sustained me nineteen days. How will I now employ
My time? That is a question that's occurred to me at work,
Which I may have neglected, sure, but I'd have been berserk

To overlook the feast of soccer running everyday . . .
Besides, it sort of is my work. You know, I need to pay
Attention to the games. It is a sports show that I host,
And I'd have been delinquent if some guy had hit the post
And I'd been sitting at my desk or talking on the phone.
But now, with no games on today, surrounded and alone,
My solace is this empty time will only last until
The Germans face the Argentines, as, happily, they will
On Friday . . . also Italy will play against Ukraine,
And then my life will bloom, as does the desert in the rain.

Trying Out

6/26/1997

Now it is truly summer.

I know this because the mail this week brought me the annual schedule of Major League tryout camps. These are day-long, open opportunities for any player between the ages of sixteen and twenty-five to demonstrate to genuine baseball scouts that he ought to be in the bigs. "Open" is the key word here, because though the only players with any shot at signing pro contracts are the youngsters who come to the camps by invitation, these worthies are invariably surrounded by dreamers and frauds.

I first attended one of the camps about ten years ago. The first alleged player I noticed had a receding hairline and a neatly trimmed gray beard. He'd brought his wife and child along to watch. He was no more between the ages of sixteen and twenty-five than Lou Gehrig is, but the scout in charge, Lennie Merullo, pretended not to notice. Also on hand was a bespectacled fellow in black, high-top sneakers, denim overalls, and a spectacularly multicolored Boston Celtics T-shirt, against which his belly strained. The rules for the camp require players to be in full uniform. This guy was in full uniform to eat half a gallon of ice cream and fall asleep under a tree, but nobody told him to go home.

The camps *are* businesslike in the sense that they all conform to the same routine: everybody runs sixty yards against a stopwatch. The outfielders try to demonstrate that they can throw. The infielders try to demonstrate that they can catch. Almost all of them demonstrate that they will never earn money by doing these things, no matter how often Major League Baseball expands.

But the dreamers don't believe it. Jodie Reed doubled the other night for Detroit, and he's about five-foot-nine . . . when he's standing on a milk crate. Cecil Fielder of the Yankees hasn't seen his toes in several seasons.

If them, why not the guys at the tryout camp? Or some of them? Or one of them. Just one who could have the day of his life and run like vintage Rickey Henderson, throw like vintage Dwight Evans, field like vintage Ozzie Smith. And even if they don't quite have that day, every gray beard—every out of uniform goof with glasses as thick as third base—can tell folks about the time he tried out for the scouts. One of the game's charms is the illusion it offers that anyone can play. It should always be so in baseball.

Coming Home

9/25/1996

The cement court is small, but it is level, and there are no cracks. A high chain-link fence prevents even the most rambunctious rebounds from kicking into the street. The steel structure supporting the backboard and the basket is impervious to fire and hurricanes. The hoop will be there after we're all dead.

I recently saw the perfect little court outside a house that will soon be for sale, and I want the house, because I must have the hoop. Long ago I let my gym membership lapse out of laziness, but I would practice on that court. Before long, I would be in shape. I would play one-on-one with my daughters, whose hands would grow, and soon they would need bushel baskets for the scholarship offers that would pour in. That's the sort of court it is.

My childhood was not deprived. There was a basketball hoop beside the driveway behind the house where I grew up. But it was all wrong from the beginning. Literally. My father and a friend of his dug the slot for the wooden post that supported the backboard. You can't dig a perpendicular trench with a manual post-hole digger. They wrestled the stanchion into the ragged hole, assured each other that it was as straight up and down as it needed to be, and poured quick-drying cement in after it. That would have been fine, I suppose, except that the concrete did not dry quickly, and at some point before it set, my father backed his Chevy Impala into the post. Then the concrete set, and ever after, every time I hit the rim or the backboard with a shot, the whole structure rocked and creaked. On windy days it moaned and stirred, even if nobody was out there playing basketball.

On that court, a long shot could begin an adventure. If the ridiculously flexible rim and backboard caught the ball just right, it would come back out like a rock out of a slingshot. There was no fence, so a rebound might end up among the daffodils, in the pricker bushes, or bouncing past the neighbor's garage. The neighbor had two boxer dogs, which sometimes roamed his yard. If they were outside, I called games on account of fear.

That would never happen to my daughters on this court I have found. It would never happen to me. Together we would play neat, solid, aggressively unidiosyncratic games . . . the games the court was built for.

Within the house alongside this court there are some bedrooms . . . I don't know how many. In the basement there is either a gas or an oil furnace . . . I don't know which. On top of the place there is a roof . . . I don't know how old it is. If you saw the court, you'd understand why I don't care.

Opening Day, 1988

Suppose that you got up this morning—
  Oh, an hour or so ago—
And suppose that you lived close enough to the ballpark . . .
  Suppose you decided to go.
And you had in your closet an old flannel shirt,
  Like the Browns and the Senators wore,
And you carried your baseball shoes out to the front steps,
  So they wouldn't scratch up the wood floor;
And you left your long shirttail outside of your pants,
  Because who's gonna see you to care?
And you walked to the ballpark (you lived that close),
  And in no time, it seemed, you were there.

And suppose now that someone (a groundskeeper, say)
  Left the clubhouse door open a crack.
So you walk right on in there as if you belong
  Past the lockers and empty bat rack
And out through the tunnel that leads to the dugout . . .
  And your spikes on the concrete . . . *clack, clack.*
The grass is as green as a king's front lawn,
  Still wet to the touch when you touch it;
The morning's so young there's a mist on the field,
  So the light there plays tricks on you such that
You see out in left field, almost in the corner,
  A ball, hooking left, toward the seats
'Til a young Sandy Amoros glides out of nowhere
  And stretches, and leaps, and completes
The catch that the Yankees still can't quite believe . . .
  And before Am'ros lands, there's the sound
Of sharp spikes in the infield that just now was empty
  And you look, and there's Ty Cobb, head down,
Roaring now around second, and heading for third,
  And the third baseman hasn't a prayer,
Because Cobb's coming harder than time or the devil
  With a snarl, and both feet in the air.

And out on the mound, at once sad-eyed and laughing,
    And thumbing his nose now at age
(He struck out major leaguers well into his fifties),
    You're dammed if it's not Satchel Paige.
And oddly, as Satchel looks in for the sign
    Old Bill Dickey is flashing his way,
You find your eyes wandering out toward deep center,
    Where Snyder, and Mantle, and Mays
Are each poised to do what each one of them did
    With such grace in those young, dead, gone days.

Go on, choose your own heroes from the dugout's top step,
    From the times you're most comfortable in:
At short, Marty Marion, Tony Fernandez;
    In the outfield, Mel Ott, Tony Gwynn.
If you're too young to summon a flying Pete Reiser,
    Then picture the rookie Fred Lynn.
Do it now, while the mist is still thick in the ballpark,
    Before the sun burns it away
And begins the next season of all our new moments . . .
    Good morning, it's Opening Day.

Opening Day, 1989

They seem stupid as stones sometimes, don't they? Dumb as dirt.
Or some of them. And we shake our heads and wonder
Did the gods, with some cosmic or comic balance in mind, divert
Intelligence elsewhere, electing not to pair it with thunder

In this one's bat, or the whip and snap of that one's arm?
And then the imp asks us, and we hide the smile,
    "What would you trade, then? What harm
Would you endure . . . to strike out the side or hit the ball a mile?"

If the devil said, "Take five batting titles, or six, or ten,
And more money than you will ever need":

But the tradeoff is this . . . again and again,
You'll tell your whole life in the papers—anyone who can read—

And even those who can't, and only watch the dots dance on TV
Will know each word you ever whispered to your lover,
Each place you ever kissed her, each degree
Of each angle of descent, each lie you used to cover

Up one from the other or the other from the one—
These are private things that keep your fans from sleep
On nights when they are lost, and cannot run,
Don't know which name to whisper in the dark and deep—

But their griefs, at least are private, their griefs, their own;
And yours will be the source of dirty jokes.
Or this: "I'll give you," says the devil, "more hits than anyone,
And not just bingles—leg doubles, too, and longer pokes

And fire to see you through the years, and such acclaim . . .
As no one since Ty Cobb has ever known.
But it won't heal you, or delight you—you'll be the same
As Cobb, who died fighting the electric bill, and died alone."

Here is the challenge for the crowd, wrapped from the boxes to the
    cheap seats—
There's dismay in the dugout, bad blood in the locker room and the
    hotel;
What will we bring it, this pleasing game that meets
Us each April, and sings and carries through our summers so well?

We're not novices here. We weren't born yesterday.
We've suffered the president who thought he could call the missiles
    back,
"I am not a crook," I heard another say . . .
And then he quit—with the election process still intact.

Likewise, today we'll be all right, we'll shrug it aside—

No problem. The charges and the counter-charges, gambling, lying,
   cheating.
Bedroom or boardroom folly, each sad or silly ride,
The old heart of the summer game's still beating;

No player's foolishness or worse, finally, does much
But spice the rich broth that sustains us on our way;
And finally the dumbest, dirtiest stories, though they touch
Us, give us pause, won't keep us from the ballpark Opening Day.

Opening Day, 1993

It should be sun-splashed, warm, and promising,
   Blue skies overhead,
It should echo with shouts and laughter,
   And hope should rise like bread.
There should be a seat for every child
   Who's never been to a game,
And the home team should win in each park today,
   No matter the home team's name.

The rookie who barely made the club
   Should go three for four with a walk;
The old guy back on a surgical knee
   Should steal third and get home on a balk.
The beer should be cold and the hot dogs hot,
   And the popcorn and peanuts free . . .
And no one should even consider the wave,
   Or watching replays on TV.

The pitchers should work without delay,
   And the hitters should step in and hit,
The umpires should be so sure on their calls
   That no one gives them . . . a hard time.

It won't be that way, not in every park,
   Not in any park, I suppose.

Instead traffic will pile up early,
    And in the cheap seats the bozos
Will rip off their shirts, though it's forty degrees
    And scream at the players below.
The reliever who cost the home team untold millions
    Will struggle, and probably blow
The save, and the manager, tired already,
    Will trudge like slow death to the mound,
And the kids will be restive and angry and cold,
    And the pitcher will stare at the ground.

The visiting team will score often and easily,
    Turning the game into a rout.
By the fourth, half the crowd will have left in disgust,
    Their summer now riddled with doubt.

We go because we don't know which it will be,
    And because, against sense, we still care.
We go to be back in the presence of baseball,
    To witness it, because it's there.
We go to renew that corn-pone continuity
    Some of us value, and, hey,
We go because fading and loss notwithstanding,
    Each year still has Opening Day.

Opening Day, 2005

Warm days are just a promise, still the games will soon arrive
On fields across the country, where the grass has come alive.
And on legs limbered up again, in jerseys crisp and clean,
The lads will once more trot on to the field. We haven't seen
Their like since last the season ended, leaving us with naught
But football and then basketball . . . two games in which I've sought
Refreshment and rejuvenation, but without a thing
That can begin to cheer the spirit like the game of spring
And summer. it's a game we cherish for its April start . . .
It melts the cramps of winter and delights the sluggish heart
Made heavy by the long, gray days, when we can only dream

Of contests in the summer's heat . . . a game that may not seem
These days as big a draw as football, or as fast a show
As hoops the way it's played in college, let alone the pros,
But still a game without which our sports calendar would lack
The long flight of the ball against the blue sky . . . that's a fact,
And lack, as well, the summer's rhythm built into the game
Of time when nothing seems to happen, 'til, as crowds exclaim
The wonder of a brilliant move that turns the game around,
And players on the field are buried in the roar of sound
That dazz'ling moment can provoke, as fans leap to their feet,
And cheer as they have not cheered since the summer past . . . the
    sweet,
Brave moment wherein old men who, for years, have calmly sat
And watched five hundred games turn and exclaim "Did you see
    that?!"
And yes, they have, because the game is simple, as it's been
But, no, they haven't, for within its frame each play can mean
A beautiful reminder of the grace—what's more to say,
The timing and the will, but more, the joy of that one play.

So now you've heard my tale and now I'm sure you'll understand
Why I'm so glad that spring's come; soccer's back upon the land.

Smelling Like Derek

8/2/2006

More evidence that there is no such thing as enough, let alone
too much, in the land of the free and the home of the brave
surfaced in New York and streaked across a stinking nation
this week when it was announced that Derek Jeter and Avon
products have teamed up to create "Driven," a fragrance that
"reflects the unique personality of one of the most driven
men in America."

That man would be the New York Yankees shortstop himself, who says that he was personally involved in the creation
of Driven, which is "a blend of chilled grapefruit, clean oak
moss, and spice."

I like chilled grapefruit as much as anybody does. Even the scent of grapefruit at room temperature delights me. I'm unfamiliar with clean oak moss, but I'm guessing it smells better than dirty oak moss. Beyond that, who can object to spice? Only a person who elects to smell bland.

Look, I'm not making this up. Derek Jeter, who, according to a recent survey by Sports Illustrated.com, was hauling in about twenty-eight million dollars a year in salary and endorsement money before the advent of Driven, is offering you, and me, and every other man who aspires to smell driven the opportunity to do so. All you have to do is buy the stuff "housed in the sleek blue bottle with the silver cap."

Though one might assume that being the shortstop for the Yankees during a pennant race would be a full time job, Derek Jeter claims he was "very involved" in creating the design of that sleek blue bottle, as well as the stuff that's inside, which his mother, Dot, and sister, Sharlee, also smelled, just to make sure it was not only "the sort of fragrance men would like to wear, but the sort of fragrance women would like them to wear."

Am I the only guy wondering whether your mother and sister would want you wearing the same scent other women might want you wearing?

And that's only one of the questions raised by Driven, which might be silly enough, but now how long is it going to be before one of Avon's wily competitors comes out with Big Lumpy, in the soft and flabby plastic squeeze bottle, for men who'd just as soon smell like Red Sox pitcher David Wells?

A Current Affair

I'm here to remind you of river swimming.

Swimming in a pool is fine, I suppose, but there is almost necessarily too much of the serious in it. Swimming in a pool is laps. Swimming in a pool is toddlers rousted out of bed at dawn, driven in carpools to the country club, then brow-beaten by some witless perfectionist of a coach about pain and gain. Swimming in a pool is burned-out, red-eyed, fifteen-year-olds who'd just as soon leave laps to their younger brothers and sisters.

Swimming in a pool is Mark Spitz, laboring—probably, even as I speak—against a stopwatch that doesn't care. Maybe you think Mark Spitz's attempt to swim in the Olympics again is brave, a stirring effort to demonstrate that you're never too old to excel. Maybe you think Spitz is simply a pathetic case of arrested development, a grown-up without imagination enough to find something better to do with his life than swim laps. Whatever. The laps he is swimming now, and the thousands more that he will swim are work. *Slap, slap,* touch, turn, kick, *slap, slap,* work.

Ocean swimming is work of another kind. Ocean swimming is a macho exercise. In the ocean, you cut through the waves, take breakers on your chest, and risk a wipeout and a mouth full of sand every time you go in deep enough to get your bathing suit wet. Ocean swimming is the sign that says "No Lifeguards on Duty." The unstated subtext is: "Take your chances, Bub, but don't blame us if you end up headed for Japan while the seagulls mock your progress."

Ocean swimming is endurance. Ocean swimmers start in England, rub grease all over their bodies, and end up in France, unless they have to be pulled—exhausted and hallucinating—into boats, in which case they weep in humiliation and swear they'll try again as soon as they can stop shaking.

Some people like to swim in lakes, but I never understood it. Lakes are, by definition, bodies of water that are dying. They are usually surrounded by picnic tables, at which huge, holiday crowds of huge people fight each other over potato chips and the last beer. Their children shriek when their wobbling Frisbees veer into the lake by mistake. This is high drama on a lake. It has always seemed to me that while the fish in the ocean are likely to be hostile and the fish in a river are likely to be energetic and clever, the fish in a lake are probably as dumb as they look. The fish in a pool are made out of plastic.

River swimming is discovering the rhythm and ride of the river and giving yourself up to it and finding that it's perfectly happy to show you the way. The river I visited recently had a number of great places to swim. My favorite was a spot where two streams came together and created a playful current that carried south for a while and then dumped you into a little eddy, where a second current would gently return you to the rock you'd slid off to begin with.

I watched a couple of ten- and twelve-year-olds play this game first. One was a girl who was pretty tentative about the whole thing, but she slipped off the flat rock, and the river caught her and bobbed her downstream, where I heard this terrific involuntary giggle. In the ocean, you hear the scream of surprise. In the lake, you hear the sigh of stupor. In the pool, you hear the gasp of lungs overworked. Give me the involuntary giggle every time.

When it was my turn, the river carried me along, too. It didn't care that I weigh more than I did in college. I was as easy on the river as the slender ten-year-old had been.

I offer all this as a public service, I guess. It's only the middle of July. The rivers are out there.

Olympic Mystery

8/25/2004

(Like millions of other people watching the Olympics, I was somewhat mystified during the gymnastics competition, when a remarkable high-bar routine by Aleksei Nemov was graded considerably higher by the crowd than it was by the judges.)

I thought we'd seen a fellow fly; I thought we'd seen him soar,
And sail around the bar with arms like cables, and, what's more,
We'd seen him leave the bar and then rejoin it with the grace

That stunned the crowd and practically electrified the place.
But then it turned out what we'd seen was something less compelling,
At least some judges thought so, 'til the whistling and the yelling
Provoked some second thoughts. I guess they felt they should rework
Their numbers if they didn't want the crowd to go berserk . . .
So as we watched, the judges scrambled, as some skeptics thought
Perhaps a couple had been leased, if not exactly bought.

The sad result of all the comic foolishness that night
Is that we end up wondering how often they are right—
These judges of gymnastics as they calculate or guess,
And wonder, too, since they have made a great routine a mess
Of muddled speculation, innuendo, and much less
Than it was when we saw it, if these judges, quite by chance
Have helped us to relearn that there's a beauty in the dance
That far transcends the politics, the medals, or the score.
Perhaps we should be grateful. They've reminded us once more
That winning's in the striving, in the will, and in the art,
And not in numbers flashed across a screen, but in the heart
Of every strong competitor who spits in time's dark eye,
And says, "Before I grow too old and slow, I'm going to fly."

I don't know who was great that night, and who was greater still,
And even if I watch the replays, hey, I never will.
But I might watch them anyway, not for a fairer shake,
But merely for the pleasure of the flying's own sweet sake.

Baseball's Pace

7/7/2004

What makes this game so different is, they play it everyday.
I know, you've heard that all before. It is, I grant, cliché,
But clichés start with something real, a fact you can't ignore:
The central fact of baseball is that there is simply more.
The season, which since April, has been grinding right along
Is only halfway over. This is neither right nor wrong . . .

It's merely different, and that's why while football coaches pace
And fellows coaching basketball are in the poor ref's face,
The managers of baseball teams are more inclined to sit
Like lumps on dugout benches, and they're more inclined to spit . . .
And less inclined to demonstrate their joy as well as sorrow,
Because they know that, win or lose, they'll play again tomorrow.
The players learn, if learn they can, that each day's winning hit
And each day's closing strikeout to preserve the win's a bit
Of history forgotten just as quickly as it's past,
And that the next game is much more important than the last,
Until it, too, is gone and nothing matters but what you
Can step into the doomed and fleeting moment, now, and do.

They play it every day, or some just sit and wait their turns
As cool nights fade from memory and summer's sunshine burns
Their noses and their necks and then, one night it's cold again,
And all the games have piled up to create a season. Then
The luckiest among them can look forward to a ring.
The rest—that's almost all of them—pack up and find that spring
Comes on a bit more quickly than it did the year before,
And they're perhaps less ready and they're just a little sore,
And later in preparing than they might have been last year,
When they were slightly quicker or their promise seemed more clear.
And then it's back to playing every day, or nearly so,
And putting every half-success behind you as you go,
And likewise every failure, for illusions like those two
Are nothing to the job you show up each new day to do.

Master Tiger

5/1997

I was s'posed to go out for the groceries this evening . . .
    I couldn't deliver the goods.
I was busy (just as I've been busy for days now)
    Thinking of Tiger Woods.
A faucet is dripping, the kids want a snack,
    And the dog needs to go for a walk.

The sink's full of dishes, the car's out of gas,
    And my wife says that we have to talk.

The yard's full of tree limbs from last week's big storm,
    And my laundry's all over the floor.
The downspout aims water right into the basement,
    And they say that it's gonna pour.

But how can I worry? And where is the meaning
    Of these dreary tasks and concerns?
I witnessed for four days on TV from Georgia
    The grace towards which humankind yearns!

Some have their philosophers, poets, and saints
    To define for them shouldn'ts and shoulds.
Not me, pal. My sign is the swoosh of the Nike;
    My mentor? The great Tiger Woods.

You may say it's early for "great" to apply,
    Or that Tiger's just playing a game.
I reply that he's greater already than any
    Phenomenon that you can name.

At twenty-one he's won a hallowed green jacket.
    He ate up the Masters for lunch.
But that's just the start. He's much bigger than sports,
    And I say this though it's just a hunch.

He's bigger than all of the Beatles together.
    He dwarfs the Colossus of Rhodes.
His gaze is hypnotic, his touch can cure lepers,
    And heal warts you've gotten from toads.

His breath is all peppermint. He has no cavities.
    Birds never spatter his car.
He's all of the myst'ries of hist'ry resolved,
    And he shoots about twelve under par.

So, bother me not with such worries as work, or
    Relationships, chattel, or goods.
From now on I spend my life free of all thoughts
    But the perfect, supreme Tiger Woods.

Tiger Loses

6/1997

They're cutting up the golf carts
    From Augusta to St. Paul
And selling them for scrap
    To iron mongers . . . that's not all.

The fairways are tomato patches.
    Roughs have gone for hay.
Latrobe out to LaCosta,
    This is golfing's darkest day.

The youngsters who'd begun the game
    Now hang out on the corner.
Each caddie, lost and mumbling, looks
    Exactly like a mourner.

The clubs are losing members,
    And their parking lots are bare.
In silent dining rooms barkeeps
    Read, doze, or comb their hair.

What's happened to this once-hot game?
    What's turned its fortunes sour?
What's crimped the hose of profit
    And made cheerful golfers dour?

What's rendered that green real estate,
    Where fell the bouncing ball,
The future site of some developer's
    Grim shopping mall?

The answer? Tiger failed. He didn't win.
   He choked. He clutched.
This boy-man among men,
   This paragon the gods had touched
And lifted to the heights
   Of golfing greatness as a lad
Became, in that last round of
   The Colonial, so bad
That he hit a shot into the water,
   Took two double bogeys,
And generally astonished
   Lots of ancient golfing fogeys
Who turned, each to the other, and said,
   "Hey, we could do that!
And we do. So what's the point?
   And each one turned just like the rat
Who leaves the sinking ship and
   Scuttles off for higher land.
And the myth of Tiger Woods fell
   Like a chip shot to the sand.

He lost. He finished fourth.
   His magic swing could not prevail.
It was as if Excalibur had cracked:
   Beyond the pale . . .

And so the wind howls cold
   Across the empty golfing links,
Where once the Tiger's legions roamed
   And bought each other drinks.

The putting greens are barren
   And the pro shops shuttered, too,
And the lesson is that Tiger's human.
   I'll be darned. Who knew?

Can golf recover? Maybe.
   If so, where? And how? And when?
It's simple. Soon as Tiger Woods
   Steps up and wins again.

Golf Hero

9/23/2006

I sing today (or write, at least) of Mr. Tateyama,
A golfer in Japan whose name's a fine rime for pajama.
You won't have heard of him, I think, although he is a pro
But Thursday he explored a realm that most will never know
No matter how much golf they play, how many shots they take . . .
Poor Mr. Tateyama made a terrible mistake
By setting out at all that day to try to play the game . . .
It may be that the world of golf will never be the same.

Upon the par-3 tee he stood. Who knows what he was thinking?
There is no evidence that in the clubhouse he'd been drinking,
But Mr. Tateyama launched his drive into the rough,
And hit his second shot astray, but that was not enough.
His third shot found some bushes far from the illusive green,
From there he whacked away until his tally was fourteen.

Yes, fourteen times did Mr. Tateyama swing his club
Against the fearsome bushes. Fourteen times the luckless schlub
Kept swinging. "I lost count," the tired golfer'd later say,
But others still were counting, and they counted all the way
To nineteen shots. That was the number Tateyama had
When he had finished up that par-3 hole. And was that bad?
Oh, that was not just bad, that nineteen was the worst, my friend.
It was the hole that Tateyama feared would never end.
And when it ended, Tateyama held a record score,
For no pro in Japan had hit a golf ball any more
Than Tateyama had, which was remarkable, 'cause, see
The hole was not par 5 or 4. That hole was a par 3.

So should we grieve for Tateyama? I don't think we should,
For out of his disaster there has come, I think, some good.

See, Mr. Tateyama never let it get him down—
I don't mean to suggest that he's a goofball or a clown,
But when the round was over, he could smile, and of the day
When on that par-3 hole he'd gone so thoroughly astray,
He said, "My mind went blank," and asked "Have I a record now?"
Yes, Tateyama, yes, you do. And so, to you, I bow.

The Unthinkable

9/8/2004

Oh, potentates have fallen, yes, and kings have been brought down,
It's true a ruler, draped with riches, can't assume his crown
Will always rest upon his head as easy as it did
When he was starting out as king . . . a callow, hotshot kid.

Still, who was not, on Monday last, unsettled by the word
That Tiger Woods was number 1 no more. It seemed absurd . . .
Consider five straight times he has been Golfer of the Year,
And four straight times he's won the money title, so it's clear
That Tiger was no fluke. He was—Childe Tiger was—a star
Who blazed across the lawns of golf one hundred under par
And seemed, we felt, near destined to continue at the top,
And then, on Monday, his reign bogeyed sadly to a stop.

Two hundred sixty-four weeks is a most prodigious run
For anyone to be the best at anything. A ton
Of golfers would give anything to be the very best
For just a day or two, to stand above the crowded rest,

And Tiger was the greatest, showered in the en'vious tears
Of golf's exalted host for just a month more than five years . . .
In five years newborns grow enough to run along to school,
In sports it's an eternity, you'd have to be a fool

To fail to understand the grand achievement Tiger wrought:
From 1999 'til now, the guy could not be caught.

It was, therefore a splendid run for Tiger and his game,
Though anyone can see that now golf will not be the same . . .
The fairways will be empty and the greens will go to seed
As termites eat the locker rooms, the country clubs will plead
For time to make the payments on their vast, palatial plots
Which will be sold off, piecemeal, for ten-thousand housing lots.
The failure of last Sunday was not merely Tiger's loss,
For Tiger's game without him at the top is merely dross.

One thing, of course, can still reverse the tumble of the game
Into a hopeless, long decline; life might go on the same
As it has gone for five years on the fairways and the greens
And on the countless number of great, glowing TV screens.
If Tiger could regain his spot atop the favored pile,
And win enough again to smile his shining Tiger's smile . . .
Until it happens all of golf's bright kingdom now will yearn
For nothing more or less than Tiger's glorious return
To number 1, which, even those who play against him know
Is where he is now meant to be, and where he must now go.

I Wish I Were a Pitcher (A Never-Changing Ode)

Oh, I wish I were a pitcher . . .
   I wish that I could throw
'em 90 miles an hour . . .
   But even were I slow,
I'd have a job in these times
   of pitchers in demand.
They'll sign you if you have a pulse.
   They'll pay you just to stand
out on the mound and look as if
   you might get someone out;
And if you do, your agent will
   emerge with so much clout . . .

And fourteen teams will bid for you
    when they hear what you've done.
They'll offer you the moon and stars.
    They'll offer you the sun.
They'll heap vast treasures at your feet
    as they hand you the pen.
(This is whether or not you ever or never
    get anyone out again.)

Boy, I wish I were a pitcher . . .
    I'd know just how to play it.
Whatever the ballclub asked me to say,
    I'd go out there and say it.
I'd wrap my shoulder up in ice,
    I'd never punch a door,
or drink in bars where there were fights,
    or denigrate the poor,
dumb, working slobs who pay the freight
    and come to watch me pitch.
I'd say they were the greatest fans,
    and I would never switch
that judgment while I worked there.
    I'd never let 'em down.
I'd swear that they were number one
    'til I was out of town.

God, I wish I were a pitcher,
    and after the game was done,
out back in the players' parking lot
    (whether I had lost or won)
the girls would swarm my car and me
    and shout and scream my name,
and beg me to let them in with me,
    but I'd tell 'em all the same:
"Can't help you, ma'am. I love my wife.
    I gotta go home and be true,

'cause Wheaties makes it worth my while
    and pays me as long as I do.
And it keeps my name on the cereal box,
    that all the managers see,
so the next time they need a pitcher,
    they'll probably call up me."

Gee, I wish I were a pitcher,
    even though it's not all cake.
I know that pitchers get hurt sometimes,
    and the pressure, for goodness sake,
is brutal if you're in a pennant drive,
    and you give up the big home run,
but even then, I bet it would be
    plenty of good, clean fun,
because win or lose, and play or sit,
    injured or strong as a moose,
they have to keep on paying you,
    unless they turn you loose.

And if they do that, you needn't fret,
    just let your agent know.
He'll find a team that wants you still,
    more than you could ever know.
And you'll sign your name,
    and they'll give you the bank,
inform the press and then
    you'll take your act on down the road
and do it all over again.

4.

Among the Memorable

In for the Duration

12/14/2005

It was not a boxing dinner, but a dinner at a college, and a guy who'd written a book set in boxing was the guest of honor, and later in the evening he would speak.

The guy is a terrific writer and he has the timing a good storyteller needs. Boxing stories are as good as any and better than most, so it was fine to be seated beside him at the dinner.

But the guy who'd written the book set in boxing was not the most compelling character at the table. That was the young woman in the wheelchair, and the wheelchair was the least of her distinctions. She wasn't eating, because of the tube in her throat, which was connected to some apparatus below the table. The tube also prevented her from speaking.

But nothing prevented her from listening, and nothing had prevented her from being at the dinner, which was unusual, because her father, who took care of her, worked long hours, and getting her into the chair, and then out of the chair and into the car, and then into the chair again was long, hard work. The guy teaching the class in which the young woman was enrolled told me that she'd never attended the class; she'd submitted her writing assignments from a computer from home. This teacher had offered his place at the table to his student and her father, and they had accepted the invitation because this was one of the nights the young woman's father didn't have to work, so there was time to get her into the car and all the rest. And as it turned out, there had been room at the table for the teacher, too. He seemed grateful for the opportunity to meet his student.

So the guy who'd written the ambitious and admirable book set in boxing told some good stories about courage and perseverance and toughness, and everybody at the table nodded appreciatively, except the young woman across the table from the writer, because she had that tube in her throat. A lot of stories about the courage and perseverance and toughness of boxers have been written by some fine writers, not just the one I was sitting next to that night, but there have not been so many stories about the courage and perseverance and toughness of someone like the young woman who sat across from the writer that night, and whose triumph was making it to the table, even though she couldn't eat, let alone tell a story, at that dinner that was not a boxing dinner.

Kirby Puckett, 1961–2006

3/8/2006

As a ballplayer, Kirby Puckett delighted even his opponents. Hall of Fame catcher Carlton Fisk said this week that Puckett brought such joy to the game that he elevated the play of everyone around him.

According to his teammates, Puckett's energy and enthusiasm were often contagious. Some of the members of the Twins, for whom Puckett played his entire, twelve-year career, used to wear T-shirts that read, "I wanna be like Puck."

Though his career was cut short by glaucoma in 1996, when he was thirty-six, Kirby Puckett accomplished plenty as a ballplayer. His Twins won two World Championships, and Puckett made the sixth game of the '91 series his personal showcase, winning it with an eleventh-inning homerun after saving it with a spectacular catch. He was a ten-time All-Star and won six Gold Gloves for his excellence as a centerfielder.

Puckett's achievement was recognized when he was elected to the Hall of Fame in his first year of eligibility, and inducted in 2001.

At the ceremony that summer, Kirby Puckett told the crowd, "I played the game and tried to live my life in a way that would make the people I love and care about proud."

During the years that followed that celebration, Kirby Puckett was far less successful at achieving that goal than he had been on the field. According to former teammate Kent Hrbek, Puckett never seemed to entirely recover from being forced out of the game. Beyond that, his extramarital affairs became public. He stopped working for the Twins. He was charged with sexual assault, and although he was eventually cleared, his capacity to generate joy gave way to self-destructive behavior. According to ESPN writer Jim Caple, who covered the Twins for portions of Puckett's career, the former ballplayer's prodigious weight gain, heavy drinking, and increasing bitterness about the absence of the spotlight he'd taken for granted had worried his friends for some time.

Kirby Puckett's career with the Twins gave his public a feel-good story about an effervescent man who made the most of his physical gifts. The years leading up to his death at forty-five demonstrated that building a life outside the game in the diminished days when the cheering has stopped can be an even greater challenge than hitting homeruns, rallying the boys on the bench, and delighting the fans.

Barry Bonds

11/17/2004

He may be baseball's greatest player . . . he may be the man
Who's hit more baseballs further than most anybody can.
He's made uncounted millions hitting balls into the bay
Adjacent to the San Francisco ball yard, but today
Would you be Barry Bonds if you could make the switch? You might.
You'd have a lot of money, so your future might seem bright,
And certainly your present would be thoroughly secure,
But for the riches and the fame you would, must needs, endure
The questions of reporters wondering are your hits ignited
By substances mysterious, and are your records blighted
Because you have conspired with the boys down in the labs
Who've engineered your biceps and your triceps and your abs?
And were you to change places with the current MVP,
Who's won the honor seven times now, you would have to be
A miserable misanthrope, suspicious, paranoid . . .
A man who would do anything he had to avoid
An interview, a question, or a photo op, a day
Upon which someone wanted to know what he had to say.

So would you, if you could, be Barry Bonds, or might you rather
Go quietly about your life and never have to bother
With monstrous expectations and with large suspicions, too,
That, taken all in all, could poison everything you do,
Until you've come to think the worst of everyone you meet,
'Cause everyone wants something, all the people from the beat
Reporter with a note pad to investigative thugs,
Who rustle through your garbage, try to peek beneath your rugs,
And learn what everybody whom you've ever known has said,
And where each nasty, brutish, short crack you have made was bred.
You might decide all that's a small price for the prize of fame
So glorious that everyone in baseball knows your name.
You might conclude you'd happily be called a bitter creep
If you could buy and sell the critics, but it is a leap
I think, to say that trading places with the MVP

Would be as pleasant now as some bright, future fall might be . . .
For clean or dirty, juiced or natural, doesn't Bonds appear
To be the least contented MVP of any year?

A Brain Is a Terrible Thing to Damage

9/29/2004

The eternal truths about boxing are that it can always get worse, and that it always does.

Last weekend's heavyweight fight in Shawnee, Oklahoma, between Riddick Bowe, who hadn't previously fought in eight years, and Marcus Rhode, who apparently will show up shirtless any time somebody will pay him to fall over, was a case in point.

Bowe, who was the heavyweight champion back before he was diagnosed with brain damage and later imprisoned for kidnapping his ex-wife, was so thoroughly out of whatever shape he'd once been in that he tried to jump on and off the scale so quickly that the officials couldn't weigh him. Mr. Rhode, Bowe's opponent, appeared to weigh approximately as much as a Lake Superior barge, but nobody cared, as long as Rhode was prepared to collapse in a heap when the bell rang. He has encouraged people to believe he will behave that way by doing so in most of his previous fights.

But back to Bowe, the star of this degrading circus. In federal court four years ago, a doctor testified for the defense that repeated punches to the head had damaged the heavyweight's frontal lobe. Bowe's decision to kidnap his ex-wife would seem to lend weight to that possibility.

But Bowe's comeback, "I never even heard of no frontal lobe before," convinced whatever shameless authority signs off on fights in Oklahoma that he was just fine.

The standard argument for boxing's legitimacy is that adults who know what they are doing and understand the risks involved in the work shouldn't be prevented from making a living with their fists, at least until even the most vile, corrupt barker can no longer sell tickets to the carnage.

It's a flimsy, discouraging excuse for licensed brutality in any case, but when one of the participants has been diagnosed with brain damage, the rationalization collapses entirely, except when the fight's in Oklahoma . . . or anywhere else where there's money to be made.

If Riddick Bowe's ongoing misadventure were unusual, it might only be the story of the shameless victimization of a damaged man. But what's happening to Bowe has happened to hundreds of confused, drooling, stumbling, blind unfortunates who've made promoters rich and provided employment for managers and boxing commissioners until the neurons in the meat shorted out so completely that those boxers couldn't answer the bell . . . a fate very likely to befall Riddick Bowe as soon as he steps into the ring against somebody who can hit him back.

Medals: Devalued, Tarnished, Absent

9/16/2004

It's tempting to say that Russian shot-putter Svetlana Krivelyova doesn't know whether to laugh or cry, except that she does know. She said this week that she feels cheated.

Ms. Krivelyova, the champion in the shot put at the '92 Olympics, finished third at the 1999 World Indoor Championships in Japan. Then the two women who finished ahead of her, Ukraine's Vita Pavlysh and Russia's Irina Korzhaneko, were disqualified when they both tested positive for the anabolic steroid stanozolol.

Svetlana Krivelyova returned her bronze medal to the International Association of Athletics Federations, but she's still waiting for the gold to which she is entitled.

In March 2004, at the World Indoor Championships in Budapest, Svetlana Krivelyova finished second to the same Vita Pavlysh who'd owed her a gold medal for five years.

Again Pavlysh was disqualified when she tested positive for stanozolol. Again Krivelyova was declared the gold medalist. Again she got no gold medal.

Finally, at the 2004 Olympics in Greece, Ms. Krivelyova, undaunted if nothing else, finished fourth. Finishing first was the same Irina Korzhaneko who'd been disqualified from the '99 World Championships. She had apparently learned nothing about moderation or masking agents, since she tested positive for stanozolol again, which meant that Svetlana Krivelyova was entitled to an Olympic bronze medal, which, of course, she has yet to see.

In sum, Ms. Krivelyova's trophy case is short three medals that will probably continue to go missing, since the two women who've got them have both, finally, been banned from competition for life, meaning they've got no incentive to cooperate with the people who run the sport.

Beyond the particulars, all this foolishness suggests that if the world of track and field isn't as corrupt and silly as we previously thought it was, it's worse; that we've finally reached a point where there's no longer any doubt that in at least one arena, elite female athletes are capable of behavior as stupid, dangerous, and crooked as their male counterparts; and that nobody who has finished fourth, fifth, sixth, or perhaps even seventh in a strength event should ever give up hope of winning—which is not to say actually possessing—a medal until the last lab test is in.

Greatness

8/6/2004

The Olympic Games in Greece will give us champions and stars, and part of the fun of the Olympics is that we can't know who they'll be. Even the television producers probably aren't sure yet.

But we do know already that these games will give us our

final opportunity to see some of the country's most successful and durable athletes play together for the final time.

Briana Scurry, Brandi Chastain, Joy Fawcett, Cindy Parlow, Julie Foudy, Kristine Lilly, and Mia Hamm will be playing in their third Olympics when the U.S. Women's Soccer Team meets the Greek team on Wednesday in Crete, two days before the opening ceremonies. Hamm, the soccer world's all-time leading scorer, has played in almost 260 matches for the national team. Kristine Lilly has played in over a dozen more.

More important to their fans than the impressive numbers is the attitude players like Lilly, Hamm, Julie Foudy and the rest have brought to their game. As members of the national team, some of them since the U.S. won the first Women's World Cup in 1991, they have been endlessly cheerfully accommodating to the public in general, and to children in particular.

It's too bad that the play of these champions and others wasn't sufficient to carry the wusa, which suspended operations a year ago. But disappointment over the suspension of the best women's soccer league in the world shouldn't detract from appreciation for what these women have done.

When they flew home, having won that inaugural World Cup in China thirteen years ago, they were greeted at the airport by one writer. One. When they played China for the World Cup in 1999, there were no empty seats in the Rose Bowl.

Beyond '99, there have been some disappointments. Where is the fan of women's soccer (or of an affordable ticket to a sports event, for that matter) who doesn't wish the wusa was still in business? But the great and lasting achievement of the women who will play together for the final time in these Olympics is that they have showed millions of people how precisely and brilliantly the game of soccer can be played, and how much enthusiasm the players can bring to the field, and how much joy they can create.

The dedication of Kristine Lilly, Mia Hamm, and their veteran teammates—the example they have set—has insured that the U.S. National Team will not lack talented players when the founding class retires. But to say the women who taught a generation to cherish their effort and enjoy their game will be missed is an Olympic-sized understatement.

W. C. Heinz

6/23/2004

In a conversation we had four years ago, Bill Heinz, one of the best writers ever to have been fascinated by boxing, celebrated his fascination by remarking on the company it put him in. "Byron was a great follower of boxing," he told me. "And so was Keats. There's nothing like a really good fight to stimulate good writing."

There must be a certain irony in being inducted into a sports hall of fame when you're eighty-nine years old.

If there is, Bill Heinz probably smiled at that irony when he was welcomed into the Boxing Hall of Fame two weeks ago, though his health prevented him from attending the ceremony.

According to the Hall's publicists, Mr. Heinz qualified for enshrinement because he wrote brilliantly about boxing. But the fact is that Bill Heinz wrote brilliantly about what it's like to be alive on the planet. Boxing was one of the many beneficiaries of Bill's curiosity, his sense of humor, his exceptional ear, and his determination to tell stories worthy of the people fortunate enough to intrigue and delight him.

Baseball was another beneficiary, and so was horse racing. Bill's dispatches from the Second World War are gems of understatement, and with a surgeon who'd served in Korea, he co-wrote the novel *MASH* under the pseudonym Richard Hooker.

I had the good fortune to meet Bill when Da Capo Press reissued some of his books, which had been out of print for years. Among the works was a 1958 novel entitled *The Professional*, which is set in boxing. *The Professional* ends in a defeat that seems surprising and unfair. The first time I met with Bill, I asked him if he'd been tempted to write a more cheerful ending.

"No," he told me, "because that's not the way it happens."

I don't watch boxing. I think the news this week that Mike Tyson, thirty-eight, intends to fight again is only the most recent bit of evidence that the alleged sport is foul in its appeal, thoroughly corrupt, and brutal beyond sensible tolerance. But if news of the induction of Bill Heinz into the Boxing Hall of Fame encourages somebody to read something Bill wrote, the result will justify the existence of the place, and it'll have to serve until somebody puts together a Writers' Hall of Fame and plunks Bill into that.

When that happens, the odds are excellent that Mr. Heinz won't take the honor—or himself—seriously. I suggest this because a couple of months ago, after I'd sent him a postcard featuring a painting by Paul Gauguin, Bill wrote in reply: "I like Gauguin, too. He was another guy who knew how to beat the old 9–5."

Alistair Cooke

4/2/2004

Alistair Cooke is celebrated as a wonderful broadcaster, and so he was.

He was also an elegant writer. In 1995 I had the opportunity to interview him about a collection of his writings that had to do with sports, among other matters. The book is called *Fun and Games.* Mr. Cooke was kind enough to read for *Only a Game* an excerpt from an essay he'd written fifty years earlier about a cricket game between Yale and Harvard.

"But after all it's not the winning that matters, is it? It's, to coin a word, the amenities that count. The smell of the dandelions, the puff of the pipe, the click of the bat, when

Harvard's batting, the rain on the neck, the chill down the spine, the slow, exquisite coming on of sunset, and dinner, and rheumatism."

Alistair Cooke and I spoke in his hotel room. He was extraordinarily gracious, and his memory was remarkable. He recalled soccer games he'd played as a schoolboy, and he spoke self-deprecatingly of his bias toward athletes who made the mastery of their difficult games look easy. My admiration for Alistair Cooke was in part based on how easy he made precision and wit seem when he wrote, and how thoroughly he seemed to be relishing not only the challenges of writing, but what had to be the chore of talking about what he'd written.

Toward the end of our conversation, I brought up the Sesame Street character Cookie Monster. Mr. Cooke's eyes shone. It turns out the master monster-maker, Jim Henson, had asked Mr. Cooke's permission to appropriate his name for "Alistair Cookie," which would give Cookie Monster himself the opportunity to host *Monsterpiece Theater*. Mr. Cooke was thrilled with the idea and pleased with its execution:

"I go into airports," he said, "and little girls, hiding behind their mother's skirts, suddenly see me and giggle, and they ask their mothers, and the mothers say, 'Yes. Go ahead. Ask him.' And they come up to me and say, 'Are you Alistair Cookie, the Cookie Monster?' I say, 'Absolutely,' and they run for their lives. So I say eighty years from now, when nobody's ever heard of *Masterpiece Theater* or John Gielgud, they'll remember the Cookie Monster, and they met him in the flesh, so I'm delighted."

Alistair Cooke's death on Monday, March 30, 2004, deprived us of an enthusiastic sports fan, a terrific writer, and a fellow who knew not to take himself too seriously . . . a man who seemed to know not only how to enjoy life, but how to convey that enjoyment—on the page or in conversation—with uncommon style and grace.

Marathon Mom

From the sunny deck behind Joan Benoit Samuelson's home in Freeport, Maine, I could see her finish her run. She wore a white T-shirt, a white baseball cap that looked too big, and loose pink shorts. No Spandex. She stopped in front of the barn that had been hauled across the lot to use as a garage ("I'm glad I wasn't in town when they did it. The people who watched were sure it would fall down"), put one hand on her hip and cocked her head to the left. Photographers have often captured her in this pose. It suggests frailty and determination at the same time. She is small and slender, and she sometimes signs her name "Joanie." She has run through injuries to her heels, her knees, and her back—and I'll stop now so this piece won't begin too early to sound like a football team's disabled list.

This particular run has been a good one, partly because last night's hard rain has washed the pollen out of the air, and partly because Joan likes running against the deadline of a commitment to do something else. She had agreed to meet me at 10:00 a.m. She had to push herself over the last miles to make it.

These days her commitments are various and legion. There is the running, of course. Apparently there will always be the running. When Bill Rodgers announced last year that he'd retired from marathoning, Joan went wide-eyed and asked him, "Bill, aren't you curious about how fast you'll be able to run one when you're fifty?" If ligaments and cartilage, the back and the heels, the ankles and the knees hold up, it's a question Joan won't have to wonder about fourteen years hence. The spirit is decidedly willing. If she isn't carrying a hundred miles a week now, she's still pushing seventy or eighty. When she doesn't put in the miles, she says she feels lazy, incomplete, and grumpy at the end of the day. As she wrote in *Running Tide*, her 1987 autobiography (with Sally

Baker), "the word *quitting* nearly gives me hives." The running, the mileage have long provided Joan Benoit Samuelson with a way to measure her worth. Even when she has not been able to win, she has been able to *work* at winning. During the increasingly long gaps between the races she has won, the work has been its own hard-earned reward.

But it has to compete for her time. Samuelson's 2:35:43 in 1993's Boston Marathon, good enough for sixth among the women, was a disappointment, but not one that she indulged for too long. "We had to get back up here fast after the race to get the peas in," she tells me, pointing out the garden between the house and Maquoit Bay. "The kids love pulling 'em up. They can relate to peas better than race results."

Marathoning and planting peas. Training runs and her turn to drive the car pool for Abby's swimming class. Physical therapy, and all the invitations to address all the groups, and the pesky inclination to try writing a children's book. These are some of the compulsions, responsibilities, and dreams that Joan Samuelson tries to balance. On this perfect early summer day, she feels as if she's established a rhythm, at least temporarily. All the balls are in the air. It hasn't always felt that way.

"When Abby was a baby," she tells me, "she had almost full-time care. Even so, I wasn't running well. And I also wasn't the mother I thought I would be. I was trying to do it all, and I couldn't delegate responsibility. Even when Martha (the nanny) was here, I couldn't go upstairs and take a nap. I should have been taking a *lot* of naps. I tried to delegate some of the letter-answering to Martha, but you know, a child writes you a letter . . . it just wasn't right for somebody else to answer it. Maybe I'm still trying to keep my fingers in too many pies, but I know what it's like to hear 'no' on the other end of the phone. I'm sensitive to it.

"But I'm really trying to establish a balance now. I try to limit my training to the morning hours, and Martha leaves much earlier than anybody else's nanny. She's told me I've probably spoiled her for working anywhere else. Abby and Anders know I'll be around and available after my run. They see my running as sort of a part-time job now. They say, 'It's good you can work while you're running, and you don't have to go to the office all day like Daddy does.' A lot of their friends have parents who both work."

Fair enough, but how many of their friends have a mom who has won an Olympic gold medal and still owns the records in a couple of marathons? "I'm not sure how much of that they understand," Joan says. "We were in New York City recently, and every time they'd see a statue in the park or a square somewhere, they'd ask, 'Who's that? What did that person do?' There's a statue of me in Cape Elizabeth, which isn't that far away. I suppose it's only a matter of time before someone who's been there tells the kids, 'Hey, we saw a statue of your mom!' I don't know how we'll handle that one."

She says she tries to be protective of the kids. At running expos or other events when people ask if they can take pictures of Joan and her family, she goes along with the idea, but it's partly because, as she says, "Abby and Anders don't have any notion why people would want a picture of me."

It's easier to keep that secret in Freeport than it would be in New York, or in Boston, or even in Falmouth, Massachusetts, where Joan Samuelson owns a 10-K race. The out-of-towners who swarm Freeport are not after pictures of the winner of the first Olympic marathon for women. They are looking for seconds at London Fog or high-water boots from L. L. Bean. Their pulses quicken with the sight of each sign that says "OUTLET," and they want bargains they can brag on when they get home. Present-day Freeport is designed to make them happy up and down Main Street and for miles either way along Route 1. It's something of a triumph that only a short distance out of town, Joan and her husband, Scott Samuelson, who handles marketing and special projects for an outfit called Woodkrafter Kits in nearby Yarmouth, have managed to establish an orderly and quiet home. Or semi-orderly and semi-quiet. It overflows with toys and stuffed animals, and the potted plants that used to be in the greenhouse are all over the deck because the greenhouse leaked and admitted ants, so the carpenters are banging away at a new one. All of which is minor-league trouble to Joan and Scott, who bought the house when it was a wreck with nothing much to recommend it but a foundation and a view. They have built it and rebuilt it from the stone on up, remodeled and rearranged it to accommodate the children, and remodeled it again after some pipes burst last winter. Now it's a wonderful, welcoming, old and new sort of place with the calm bay out the kitchen window. It is, in short, the sort of place where a former world champion might contemplate in contentment her past glories, the present blessings of her healthy children and devoted husband, and the myriad projects that fascinate her and don't require a warm-up of eighty to a hundred miles of roadwork each week.

Or it might be if the former world champion were anyone but Joan. "Something that I'm thinking about seriously is 1996 in Atlanta," she says, "the Olympics on home soil again." Somewhere alarm bells clang, but not for Joan. We may not want to hear it, anymore than we wanted to hear Willie Mays say he intended to play another season, or Muhammad Ali say he'd signed for another fight, but Joan, too, has another dream. "I don't necessarily think I could go out there and win a gold medal again," she says, "but I think I can be competitive with the best in the world. I think if I could put this day-to-day responsibility behind me, within two or three months I could gear up for something that could potentially mean a lot to me. I think the focus and the drive are still there. I just have to find that time frame and dedicate my energies in that direction. By '96 the children will be a little bit older, and they'll understand what I'm doing and how I'm devoting my energies to that goal."

Gone are the echoes of the talk earlier in the day about scar tissue, electrolyte imbalance, and the acceleration of fluid loss as the body grows older. "I just don't *feel* like I'm old," Joan says and later, "Don't misunderstand me. I remember a couple of years ago when either Jimmy Connors or John McEnroe talked about regretting that his children couldn't see him play his best tennis. Whichever of them it was said he wished his kids could have known him at the peak of his game. I've said to myself, 'Do you wish that?' And deep down I really don't think I do, because I'd rather see my children mainstreamed into society, knowing that you can go out and do something great and still have a life that's routine and normal and balanced. Would I want to see my kids running in my footsteps? I'll get a bigger kick out of a piano recital or a painting. When they had parents' day at Abby's swimming class, she jumped into the deep water for the first time, and I leapt off the bench and cheered. Then I sat down quick with my hand over my mouth. I felt like one of those Little League parents."

So it would not be for them. If Joan Benoit Samuelson traded the balance that has been so hard-won for the single-minded discipline and relentless training that might lead to another run in the Olympics, it would be for her. It would be to test herself again as she has always tested herself, for a reason more fundamental than the need for fame or money that might drive another runner. Early in her 1987 autobiography, she wrote, "The goal I can neither reach nor let go of is out there somewhere. I dread meeting it."

It's perhaps unfair to lift that line from its context. Elsewhere in *Running Tide* she wrote, "Winning isn't everything, and it isn't the only thing. It is one of many things." She also quotes an aphorism that she heard Elie Wiesel attribute to Rebbe Pinhas of Koretz: "If someone finds it necessary to honor me, that means he is more humble than I. Which means he is better and saintlier than I. Which means that I should honor *him*. But then, why is he honoring me?" These words suggest a perspective on her own career and sports in general that has eluded all but a very few U.S. athletes between the ages of four and dead. It's a perspective that has its beginnings in one of the healthiest and most sensible childhoods imaginable. An excellent and devoted skier and a prizewinning runner even as a child, Joan was taught early that schoolwork and chores came before sports. On Sunday everybody went to church before hitting the ski slopes, though it was okay to wear your ski boots and parka at early Mass. As a child, she says, "I learned to put something besides myself at the center of my universe. I was also taught to love myself, but to strive to be a better person. And I came away knowing when to laugh."

Winning an Olympic gold medal didn't diminish that latter capacity. Three years after L.A., Joan suggested to her publisher that her autobiography really ought to be entitled "Out on a Limp." But the dream and determination that still drive her running spring from some source beneath laughter. Despite injuries and time they are the persistent and relentless voices that drown out what most objective observers, especially those who do not run, would consider common sense. Within one extended conversation on a sunny summer morning, Joan can say of last spring's Boston Marathon, "I lost the race at 9:00 a.m. I was dizzy the day before in the humidity. I thought, 'You're the mother of two. Do you want to put your life in jeopardy?'" and then, "I may try to run one when I'm fifty."

At thirty she acknowledged that because of the damage running had done, she could not walk properly unless she was wearing shoes. At thirty-six she talks convincingly of a plan that would earn her a spot in the '96 Olympics. Sometimes she asks herself if what she has done and what she is doing will diminish the rest of her life by making it impossible for her to run recreationally in ten years, or five, or two. In her autobiography she put the question to rest by saying, "Every step I take pushes me further into the mystery."

Now the mystery is more crowded than it was then. The runner is no longer just Joanie, whose mother was once so horrified at a newspaper photograph of her daughter at the end of a race that she wrote, "If this is what marathoning makes you look like, please stop." Now she is Mrs. Samuelson, mother of two, and Abby and Anders are in the mystery, too. Mom is balancing things daily and trying, sometimes on battered tiptoes and beat-up heels, to see over the horizon, where the blueprint for the next balancing act may already be sketched out.

At the end of our allotted time, precisely when Joan has said it would happen, Abby and Anders come in. They are shy in my presence for about ten seconds. Then Anders shows me the books he's brought home from the library, and Abby asks us all if we've seen her bug box. After a short search, the box turns up, and Abby says she's off to fill it with creatures.

"Abby," says her mother, "I saw a lot of butterflies when I was running this morning. You could find some in the garden right now."

"This is a bug house," says Abby.

"I know," Joan nods, "but your butterfly net is right out on the deck. You could put the butterflies in here."

"I just want some bugs," says Abby. Her mother can have the butterflies.

I leave with spinach and radishes from the garden and an invitation to come back some other summer day with my own family, just for the fun of it. I drive south toward my own mystery and balancing act and hope against long odds that the decisions Joan Samuelson will make down the years will be natural, easy, pain free, and triumphant. You're not supposed to cheer in the press box, but what the hell? I'm no beat man. The end of the story is an odd place for a disclaimer, but here it is: Regarding Joan Benoit Samuelson, I'm rooting for victory on all fronts—more wins and balance like only someone superhuman can achieve and sustain, butter-flies *and* bugs, quiet pride in solid achievement at home and all around the dinner table where everyone will continue to always eat together, more contentment and acceptance than those among us who embrace the work and solitude that winning demands have any right or reason to expect.

Goodbye, WUSA

9/17/2003

When a sports league suspends operations after three seasons, it's easy to conclude that the enterprise was a mistake from a business point of view.

John Hendricks and the rest of the founders of the WUSA assumed that the excitement evident as the 1999 World Cup tournament moved toward its extraordinary conclusion and the joyous rush of the championship game had built an audience, and that with that audience, or at least the promise of it, the league would draw corporate support. Mr. Hendricks was, as he acknowledged in his announcement of the suspension of the league, "intoxicated" by that possibility.

But to conclude that the WUSA was a failure in anything but a business sense suggests a lack of appreciation for what the teams and players in the league became to the girls and boys and men and women who attended the games. Critics of the play on the field knocked the best female players in the world for not being as strong or as fast as the best male players in the world. More thoughtful observers saw in the women's game the finesse, precision, and imagination that makes soccer beautiful. That was sufficient reward for the price of what was, for many people, the only affordable ticket in town.

But there was more. The women who made the league happen three years ago and those who joined them over the next couple of seasons are not only accomplished athletes. Many of them are also articulate, personable young women who demonstrated in practice and during games the joy they'd found in their work, which was, for long, brilliant stretches, indistinguishable from their play. They reminded those fortunate enough to witness their games and get to know them even just a little that pro athletes don't have to be defensive and distant, let alone smug, narrow-minded, self-absorbed, or aggressively vulgar.

Joe Cummings, the general manager of the Boston Breakers, told me that several of the players called him on Monday afternoon, shortly after the announcement that the WUSA was closing up shop, to ask "What could we have done?"

The answer is, "Nothing more." In a land where bigger just isn't better, it's the only option . . . a land where if you're not on commercial television, you're unworthy of notice, and a land where grace won't outdraw gore, you couldn't have done any more than you did. Shame on us that while it was plenty, it wasn't enough.

Navratilova Crowns Her Career

1/29/2003

Martina Navratilova won the first of her 342 professional tennis titles thirty years ago. She was sixteen.

She won the most recent of those titles at a major tournament last weekend, when she and partner Leander Paes, who took his first breath thirty years ago, knocked off Todd Woodbridge and Eleni Danilidou, 6–4, 7–5, to become the mixed-doubles champs at the Australian Open.

Mixed doubles is the poor relation of pro tennis, an event that many of the successful players of both genders don't bother to enter because they assume the last stages of the tournament will find them concentrating on winning the headline events. Still, this particular mixed-doubles title was well worth the trip to Melbourne for Navratilova. Now, eight years after winning her most recent title at a major tournament, she has won every title available at Wimbledon, the U.S. Open, the French Open, and the Australian Open.

That achievement may mean less to purists than, for example, Martina's nine Wimbledon singles titles. But at forty-six, thirteen years past her most recent Wimbledon triumph and technically long-retired, Navratilova has crowned her career with a remarkable symmetry.

It's kind of cute that tennis offers players three ways to win a title in each major tournament: singles, doubles, and mixed doubles. It's also neat. Several other sports offer competitors multiple opportunities of various sorts: swimmers and runners can, of course, compete in more than one event, including relays. A light-heavyweight boxer or a deluded middleweight champ can bulk up and compete for the big kids' title . . . or titles. But opportunities and triumphs within those sports are ragged, impossible to quantify.

Martina Navratilova can sit back, put up her well-traveled feet, and think on the fact that since tennis became a big deal—that is, a professional sport—nobody else has done what she has done, and there is not a distinction at a major event which has not been hers.

It can be argued that tennis is a small and insular world, but who can argue about the most remarkable achievement within that little space?

Pat Summitt

3/23/2005

The number is 880, and some of the story is in the number.

As of Tuesday night, no basketball coach has guided a team to more wins than Pat Summitt of Tennessee. Dean Smith is now second.

There are lots of other impressive numbers associated

with Pat Summitt's coaching career. Her teams have built a winning percentage of .837; since the women's tournament began in 1982, Tennessee has appeared in every one of them and built a record of 87 wins against just 17 losses; the Vols have never lost in round one or round two. Summitt's teams haven't been just consistent; they've been consistently excellent.

Tennessee proudly trumpets another number: the graduation rate for Summitt's players who have stayed at Tennessee throughout their eligibility and, as the public relations people in Knoxville put it, "honored their commitment," is 100 percent. The NCAA counts a little differently, but Tiffany Carpenter, who handles public relations for the athletic department at Tennessee, maintains that the figure for Tennessee's basketball-playing females last season was 75 percent only because when Tasha Butts exhausted her eligibility, she told Coach Summitt that she was going to drop out to play in the WNBA.

"No," Summitt explained. "My graduation rate is 100 percent, and you're not going to spoil it."

Summitt made Butts a graduate assistant, and this year, according to Tiffany Carpenter, Butts is finishing her degree.

But perhaps the most extraordinary numbers associated with Pat Summitt's achievement are the ones that remind us where she and her program and women's college basketball in general were when Summitt took the job at Tennessee thirty years ago. Now, of course, the women's game provides scholarships, fills gyms with paying customers, generates a sizeable TV audience, and sends a new class of talented players to the WNBA each summer.

When Pat Summitt won her first game at Tennessee on January 10, 1975, the number of scholarship athletes on her team was zero, and the fans in the seats numbered fifty-three.

Pat Summitt's Raise

5/24/2006

It seems to me it might be nuts for anyone to get
A million dollars just for coaching basketball, and yet,
A lot of guys have gotten more for coaching lots of things,
And leading teams that haven't led the league in winning rings.
(You cannot hire a football coach at any football school
For less than millions, and you'd have to be an utter fool
To fail to understand a worthy coach is what you need
To hide the fact that some guys they recruit can barely read.)
But I digress. Pat Summitt is the newest millionaire
Among the coaching ranks, and it's a fact that we should care,
For Summitt has been coaching now for thirty-two long years,
And when she started, she was bouncing checks, and while her peers
Among the men then coaching men had scholarships to give,
Pat Summitt called her parents for the dough on which to live.

But now she's won nine hundred games, her Vols are on the map,
And if Pat Summitt's landed now in fortune's very lap
Of luxury, it is perhaps a part of the acclaim
That's come at last and lately to adorn the women's game.
In that regard, more power (and more money) to the she
With sixteen Final Fours, who has built up at Tennessee
A program known for winning, yes, six times they've won it all.
Why shouldn't she receive a million bucks for coaching ball?
She's made the name of Tennessee synonymous with winning . . .
Where otherwise it would be Davy Crockett's first beginning
And little more. All right, I'm kidding, still Pat Summitt's made
A household name of Tennessee, and now she's being paid
Accordingly, and if you think that's silly anyway
Consider that at Tennessee, where in the fall they play
A game called football, Phillip Fulmer—not a name you've heard
I'm not surprised, I must admit, to me it seems absurd . . .
For Fulmer is the football coach. I'm sure he's good at that . . .
But good enough for him to make a million more than Pat?
Because he gets a tad more than two million every season,

Which, in this whacky world of sports, might lead someone to reason
That Summitt, at the summit of a world that she has made
At just a million bucks a year is vastly underpaid.

U.S. Women Win

4/13/2005

The great temptation is to say that it couldn't have happened
to a nicer guy, because there is no nicer guy in sports than Ben
Smith, who coaches the U.S. Women's Ice Hockey Team.

But the World Championship that the U.S. women won in
Sweden on Saturday didn't happen to Ben Smith, any more
than it happened to Angela Ruggiero or Katie King or any of
the other women who've banged away at Canada in this tournament since it began fifteen years ago. Losses happen to
people, not wins. In '98, the U.S. women beat Canada in the
Olympics, but eight times the Canadians and the Americans
had met in the final of the World Championship tournament, and eight times the U.S. women had come away with
silver medals.

"These are two pretty hard-driven teams," Ben Smith said
after this year's final. "It seems, over the years, that we've
been able to bring out the best in each other."

"Seems? I know not seems." Even as Sweden and Finland
and a few other teams have waxed and waned, sometimes
briefly seeming almost good enough to challenge the world's
two best, every final has pitted the United States against
Canada. Like the championship games in 1997 and 2000,
Saturday's match went to overtime, but this one more seriously cranked up the "bring out the best in each other" business. Neither team scored in sixty minutes of regulation.
Neither team scored in a twenty minute overtime session. By
that time Canada's keeper, Kim St. Pierre, had turned away a
remarkable forty-nine shots, and that didn't count the ones
that had clanged off the post or skidded across the crease.

The scoreless overtime meant the championship would

come down to a shootout, and in that tense affair, the U.S. women tucked in three goals to Canada's one.

In the pictures of celebrating players, it's impossible to say who is the happiest member of the U.S. team. All the smiles are wide, all the eyes are bright. But for anyone who's been paying attention to this remarkable group of women for any length of time, it's hard to avoid singling out the indefatigable Cammi Granato for special recognition. She's been a member of the team since the team came into being fifteen years ago. Among her current teammates is a young woman who was two when Granato first pulled on a USA jersey. Ben Smith and fans of the women's game have known for a long time now that Cammi Granato is a winner. Now the folks who only check out the back pages in the sports section and thumb through the record books know it, too.

Cammi Granato Cut

8/31/2005

Last year, Mia retired. Last week, Cammi was cut.

"Great players are left behind when teams are selected," said Women's National Ice Hockey Team Coach Ben Smith. "This team is no different than any other team."

In this case, maybe he was just a little wrong. Cammi Granato, thirty-four, has been the spine of the women's national team as long as there has been a women's national team. She was the captain of both the 1998 aggregation that won the first Olympic gold medal in women's ice hockey, and the 2002 squad that came second to Canada in Salt Lake City. She lasted long enough to play on the team that finally beat Canada for a world championship this year, and she scored forty-seven goals in nine world tournament appearances to complement her ten Olympic goals.

Cammi Granato began playing hockey at five, and like all the women who embraced the sport beginning decades ago, she played with and against the boys. She used what might have been regarded as a disadvantage to make herself a stronger player. "If I was average," she has said, "people wouldn't accept me. If I was better, they'd respect me."

Ben Smith, who ran the men's team at Northeastern University before becoming the head coach of the women's national team in 1995, has said that when a men's team loses a player, those who remain shrug and assume the team will be better, but when a women's team loses a player, her former teammates mourn the loss of a friend. I asked Ben on Tuesday whether there was mourning among his players now.

"Oh, yes," he said, "and I've had to deal with it myself. I've never coached a player that long. She was on the '95 team when I came into my first camp as a coach. She was one of the players who stood up and said, 'Hey, this guy's okay.'"

In sports, everybody who doesn't quit gets cut. Cammi Granato never quit, and when she got cut, she handled the disappointment with the grace those of us who've known her expected. She said she was proud of the women who'd made the team.

Still, as the U.S. team plays in the Four Nations Cup in Finland this week, it's a little hard to know whether to feel sorrier for Cammi, who wanted so badly to make the trip, than for Ben, who had to tell her she was staying home.

Hockey's Happier Story

4/27/2005

There is every chance that the winter of 2004 and the spring of 2005 will endure as the dumbest, most deplorable chapter in the history of the National Hockey League, and that's no small achievement. This is a league long-characterized by the tacit agreement between the players and owners to embrace aggravated assault as part of their entertainment package . . . a league in which the absence of cold weather instantly qualifies a region as a target for expansion . . . a league in which an executive and promoter once doubled as an agent, the better to swindle gullible players out of their salaries and investments.

Over the past winter and spring, the players and owners have partnered to create a debacle so spectacularly embarrassing that Bobby Orr himself wrote a column in Sunday's *Lawrence Eagle Tribune* to characterize their posturing as nonsense, and warned that "our sport is in danger of becoming irrelevant."

Happily, he's wrong. The NHL may become irrelevant, but hockey's still a lot of fun and fun is always relevant. Even in this non-season of the NHL, lots of folks know this. Among them are the people who make up the Hockey Humanitarian Foundation, a group that presents an annual award to the college hockey player deemed the game's "finest citizen."

Earlier this month, the 2005 award went to Sarah Carlson, a senior at Boston College. A two-time captain of the hockey team, Carlson was named this year to both the hockey east first team and the New England Hockey Writers' Women's Division I All-Star Team.

But the papers are full of first teamers and all-stars. They are not so full of college students who've traveled to Mexico to help build a church, worked with disabled children at a summer camp, and organized a sled hockey game as a fund-raiser for kids with disabilities. They are not rife with stories about college athletes who've devoted their time to after-school programs for disadvantaged children and volunteered for food and clothing drives, taking time out only to work with a paralyzed athlete in a city hospital, and then organize their teammates to visit disabled children.

If time permitted, I could go on, because Sarah Carlson did, for four years, all the while not only playing hockey, but also excelling as a student in BC's nursing program.

I'm a little late with this note of recognition. Sarah Carlson received her hockey humanitarian award three weeks ago. But after a winter and spring as bad as these have been for the NHL, maybe it's never too late for an encouraging hockey story.

Sorenstam the Great

6/15/2005

The excitement of the games should be sufficient. We should be satisfied, if not thrilled, to see the most talented and dedicated athletes compete with each other.

But it isn't, and we're not.

That's why every other prize fight is billed as the battle of the century, and baseball match-ups are regularly marketed as fabled, eternal rivalries.

And then, perhaps just often enough to remind us that adjectives like "incredible" aren't quite always out of place on the sports page, an athlete turns in a performance or a series of performances that alters the way we understand his or her game.

These days, Annika Sorenstam is that athlete. Not only has she won six of the eight LPGA golf tournaments in which she has competed this spring, she has done it as if nobody should have assumed the possibility of any other result. Having won last weekend's LPGA Championship, she is halfway to accomplishing the goal she set for herself before the season began: winning the four major tournaments that constitute her sport's grand slam. More remarkably, she is so thoroughly dominating golf that for her to lose either of the two remaining tournaments would constitute an exceptional upset.

Baseball teams go on winning streaks all the time. The Miami Dolphins once played an entire football season without losing a game. From 1959 through 1966, The Boston Celtics won eight NBA Championships in a row. But golf isn't supposed to work that way. Since taking a shot at a PGA tournament two years ago, Annika Sorenstam has won nineteen of the thirty-eight events on the LPGA tour. That's half. And of course this spring she has pushed that proportion to three-quarters. She is so far ahead of the field in her profession that the other women on the tour have begun to joke that the only way one of them will win is if Sorenstam forgets to sign her scorecard.

The silliest consequence of Annika Sorenstam's exceptional accomplishment is the emergence of a question: Is Sorenstam's dominance good for the game?

Good for the game? It expands our minds. It enlarges our expectations. It surprises us and increases our delight. Good for the game? Annika Sorenstam's ongoing performance on the golf course is good for our imaginations. In these days of calendars far too crowded with games, how many results can lay claim to that distinction?

The Beauty of a Diminished Thing

7/6/2005

A year ago at the 2004 Olympics, the U.S. Women's Soccer Team won a gold medal.

Two years ago, on exceptionally short notice, the U.S. hosted a successful Women's World Cup . . . especially successful for the German team, which won it.

For the three summers previous to that tournament, the WUSA, now defunct or just resting, depending on the level of your credulity, delighted a fan base consisting, it turned out, of a disproportionate number of cheering children and their delighted parents, and fatally lacking in corporate partners.

In this summer during which the MLS regular season is joined by World Cup qualifiers, Gold Cup matches, and visits by Real Madrid, Manchester United, A.C. Milan, and Fulham, A.C., among other worthies, the calendar for the women's team is limited to friendly matches like the one on Sunday in Portland, Oregon, against Ukraine.

Which is not to say the women's team has not been generating news. Late last month, Coach Greg Ryan cut Brandi Chastain, who won the 1999 World Cup Final with her penalty kick. Ryan welcomed back Tiffany Milbrett, who had cut herself from the squad nearly two years earlier because she felt then-head coach April Heinrichs had taken the fun and spontaneity from her game. Against Canada earlier this summer, Milbrett appeared in her two hundredth game for the national team. Because she nearly always scores in Portland, it's likely that on Sunday she will pot her one hundredth goal.

Before the U.S. team gathered for training and summer friendlies, Milbrett had been playing in Sweden, as had veteran Kate Markgraf and super veteran Kristine Lilly. The sad aspect of that circumstance is that there is no longer a pro league to employ them—and the rest of the world's best players—in this country. The upside of the story is that Lilly, who will play in her 297th game for the U.S. team on Sunday, has reported that playing in Sweden was delightful. There is no reason to doubt her, and nobody who has seen the national team perform or who followed the WUSA through its three seasons will be surprised that these veterans, unlike Mia Hamm and Julie Foudy, have elected to continue playing despite the absence of a U.S. pro league and the fact that the next World Cup, which will be held in China, is still two years away.

Most of us won't see the games, these friendlies, this summer, but it's encouraging to know that the joy is still in them.

Lilly's Three Hundredth Game

1/18/2006

The talk is all of football as the playoffs grind along,
Or basketball, as Duke does very little that is wrong,
And Tennessee, is likewise playing brilliantly these days,
But shouldn't there be mention of a woman who still plays
Her game without distraction, though her peers have all retired?
Her game is mocked by dunderheads, although it has inspired
Excitement in the world beyond our narrow-minded land . . .
But I digress. My point is we should now strike up the band

To celebrate a milestone that must amplify the fame
Of Kristine Lilly. Now she's played in her three hundredth game.

Three hundred games. Nor has she merely played: she's also scored
Five score and five goals in those games. And she has been adored
By legions of the children for whom she has signed her name.
When she hangs up her soccer shoes, the game won't be the same . . .

But then she might not ever do it. Hey, she's thirty-four
And going strong. She may well play a couple hundred more,
And wouldn't it be foolish to assume that should she do it,
She'd slow down in the process and just saunter her way through it?
Because this week in China, playing Norway for a cup,
Kris Lilly scored the goal with which the U.S. team went up
One-nil. Nor did she then decide to cease or to desist;
Indeed, upon the second goal she tallied the assist.

She's once more on a winner in a sport where playing must
Fulfill the needs of those who play. Although it isn't just,
There is no women's pro league now; they play for joy and pride,
And no one's made of that endeavor any better ride
Than Kristine Lilly, breaking records every time she plays,
And showing time it can't prevail in every player's days.

Brazil

6/14/2006

The Germans are relentless and the Portuguese can slide
The play across the field with fluid motion, like a glide
Across a shining dance floor. Argentina strikes with flair;
And Italy's dramatic when the contact isn't there.
But what care I for all these teams when I behold the thrill
Of watching soccer as it's played by players from Brazil?

Australia thumped Japan to earn perhaps their only points,
And Sweden, highly rated, aches in spirit and in joints . . .
For they could not prevail against the tiny island nation . . .

Ah, Trinidad-Tobago, for a moment a sensation.
But these are merely subplots, mere distractions, if you will,
For that which has united us: the worship of Brazil.

The U.S. fumbled blindly through the Czech Republic game,
And now their fans, consumed with loathing, don't know
    whom to blame . . .
Some say the coach and others lack of energy or plan,
Still others look ahead and say if anybody can
Beat Italy, the U.S. team perhaps will be the one,
If they remember how to shoot and tackle, pass, and run.
But all the talk of next games, every promise that they'll thrill
Must take, I fear, a backseat to the glories of Brazil.

The Netherlands are sturdy, England's likely to endure,
And Mexico has started well and should go through for sure . . .
The French may yet recover from their draw against the Swiss,
Croatia likely wins their next two games, but should they miss
The second round, they'll still have had the everlasting thrill
Of sharing the same soccer pitch with players from Brazil.

Am I too much enamored of the yellow-shirted team
That plays as if it had transformed the game into a dream
Of grace, imagination, and a rare, contagious glee?
If so, I won't apologize, because it seems to me
That worthy is the side that has prevailed and prob'ly will
Again and then again. How can one root against Brazil?

5.

Sports Misused, and Games as Solace

Wars and Circuses

2006

If we go to war somewhere else, where will Major League Baseball put the next patriotic song?

The national anthem was first sung at a Major League Baseball game in 1918, and since 9/11 and the bombing of Iraq, part two, we've had "God Bless America" during the seventh-inning stretch. It fits comfortably, since fans have always been accustomed to a pause in the action there.

If the United States invades Iran or North Korea or Venezuela, where do we put the next martial selection? Three and a half innings in?

The trappings of jingoism have been part of the Super Bowl for all forty of its years: military bands, color guards, multi-gun salutes, ear-splitting flyovers by the Blue Angels, the "bombs bursting in air" . . . it's hard to imagine the big game without the explosive soundtrack.

If you're uncomfortable with the songs imploring God to bless America in its latest military misadventure, you might remain seated during the anthem(s). And then you might get punched in the head by the patriot in the row behind you.

For some, the overt coupling of sports with politics has been no joke. When the first President Bush took the country to war against Iraq, college sports teams added an American flag patch to their uniforms. One of the players expected to wear the flag was Marco Locar, an Italian playing basketball for Seton Hall University. Locar told his coach that as a Christian and a pacifist, he opposed the bombing and the war, and preferred not to wear the flag, since as far as he could tell, it had come to represent support for the war.

That stand was fine with Locar's coach and his teammates; the kid wasn't even an American. But it was not fine with the Americans who filed into Madison Square Garden on the night Seton Hall played St. John's. Many of them jeered Locar every time he touched the ball. Shortly thereafter, he began receiving hate mail, which upset his pregnant wife enough to convince Marco Locar that he should quit school and return to Italy.

That triumph of fatheads was shameful, but at least nobody got killed. Such is not always the case when our games are dragged to war. In an attempt to cover the most recent invasions with glory, the administration of Bush II attempted to celebrate the enlistment of Pat Tillman, late of the National Football League's Arizona Cardinals, as proof that going to battle in Afghanistan and Iraq was a heroic enterprise, since a man the American public regarded as a hero—a pro football player—was doing it. When Tillman, who had turned his back on a multimillion dollar National Football League contract to serve in the military, was killed in Afghanistan, "millions of stunned Americans mourned his death and embraced his sacrifice as a rare example of courage and national service."[1]

This response turned out to be grotesquely ironic on a couple of levels.

First, Tillman appeared to have had no interest in promoting the administration, the war, or himself. He felt serving his country as a soldier was his duty under the circumstances, and his intention was to go to war as unobtrusively as it is possible for a pro football player to go to war, a preference for which those attempting to use him had no respect.

Then there was the muddle surrounding his death and lies it spawned. In April of 2004, Tillman's platoon left its base near the Pakistan border to look for Taliban fighters. A little over a week into that mission, Tillman was reported dead, the victim of enemy fire. On April 30, the U.S. Army Special Operations Command released a statement that said Tillman had encountered the enemy, "directed his team into firing positions and personally provided suppressive fire."[2] Tillman was posthumously awarded a silver star for valor.

At the time that version of the events leading to Pat Tillman's death became public, the Army knew that it was a self-serving lie. Over the next few months, thanks in part to the determination of Tillman's parents to learn the truth about their son's death, it became apparent that he had been killed by so-called "friendly fire" in the sort of gruesome accident that teaches us over and over again that for the people doing the fighting, war is chaotic and indiscriminately deadly. Eventually the army acknowledged that Pat Tillman died because U.S. troops "failed to positively identify their respective targets and exercise good fire discipline,"[3] which sounds like military-speak for "it was dark and noisy, and everybody was scared and confused as hell, so they started shooting at everything they could see, as well as some things they couldn't see."

Pat Tillman's choice to enlist was no less remarkable for the way his life ended. Very few athletes walk away from lucrative contracts to risk their lives in combat. But it's comforting to imagine that his ghost nightly haunts the opportunists who tried to turn his terrifyingly random and accidental death into propaganda that would portray fighting in Iraq in terms of "that old Lie: Dulce et decorum est / Pro patria mori,"[4] thereby encouraging other young men, particularly those inclined to choose a pro football player for a role model, to sign up.

Sportswriters have long written about our games in military terms. A season is a campaign, a long pass is a bomb, a game that drags on and beats up players on both sides is a war. Likewise those in the military have often resorted to the language of sports to describe what they've been doing. One of the first pilots interviewed after the bombing of Baghdad directed by Bush the First said of the surprisingly easy mission, "It was like being a pro athlete heading into his first game, but then the other team didn't show up."

In fact, it's silly at best and often obscene to describe even the most violent and destructive games in terms of war. Pro football, for example, tears its players apart, drives them to gobble dangerous and unpredictable drugs, and renders the heaviest of them susceptible to early death, all so fans can enjoy a spectacular circus. But a death during a pro football game is a shock.

Death during a war, whether at the hands of the enemy or as a result of "friendly fire," is simply what happens. Civilians upon whom bombs are dropped know that. So do veterans. A lot of soldiers in a lot of wars have reported being *astonished that they weren't killed.*

Our games are defined in part by rules prohibiting gratuitous violence. A linebacker who slams into a running back and drives him to the ground with enough enthusiasm that the running back gets up slowly and wobbles in circles as he tries to find his way back to the huddle is celebrated. But if the same linebacker grabs the face mask on the running back's helmet and twists his head like a cowboy trying to bring down a steer, the tackler's team is penalized fifteen yards.

Some of our soldiers who operate outside the rules of war established by the Geneva Convention and other agreements are penalized, but most aren't, and those violations and penalties occur in an insane context for which sports offers no correlative. The U.S. government prosecutes a half-bright soldier photographed with a naked detainee on a leash, and congratulates itself for holding the U.S. soldier to a higher standard of behavior than that to which soldiers abusing prisoners and civilians under another banner are held. But who's disciplined for the bombing raid that kills a dozen Pakistani citizens guilty of nothing but living in a village where a suspected terrorist might have spent the previous night?

Rules define games like football, basketball, and hockey. Without them, the games would be mayhem. War is mayhem, without rules. It is chaos. No army has ever been free of commanders who shrug off the slaughter of innocents as unfortunate but necessary, and soldiers who become frightened or frustrated enough to shoot at whatever their adrenaline, fear, and frustration leads them to imagine.

But at home, many of us root for U.S. soldiers the same way we root for our favorite college football teams. "We Support the Troops" ribbons in various colors decorate bumpers alongside the "Go Huskers" and "Fighting Irish" stickers.[5] There may seem to be a parallel here. Maybe the same people who support Nebraska football even when the players are being arrested for assault support the troops in general as well, no matter what specific acts of sadism in the prisons presided over by those troops have recently come to light. But again the comparison is silly. College athletes represent their schools, or at least the boosters who pay for the programs whose colors they wear. When one of the players is caught stealing a car or using illegal drugs or dragging a woman down a flight of stairs by her hair, the athlete might be disciplined and the college's athletic program may be temporarily inconvenienced by the loss of a few scholarships, but everybody who follows the college game recognizes these felonies and misdemeanors and consequent slaps on the wrist from the National Collegiate Athletic Association as the cost of doing business for a team that wishes to compete at the highest level. Soldiers, on the other hand, represent their country, and in the case of the United States, it's a country in which most citizens are apparently convinced that their military is more righteous, better behaved, and less inclined toward irrational or vicious conduct than are the soldiers of other countries. Perhaps Americans have to believe that in order to think that they are entitled to whatever they can afford to buy in general, and to cheap oil in particular, and that any action taken in the service of that credo, especially if it's advertised as the democratization of the oil-rich invadee for its own good, is worthy of their support.

When they are rooting for a football, baseball, or basketball team, most fans are unencumbered by that sort of baggage. When Larry Lucchino, the President and CEO of the Boston Red Sox, referred to the New York Yankees as "the evil empire," only idiots took him seriously, and even Lucchino eventually laughed . . . and then indicated he was sorry if he'd offended anyone. It was the goofy remark of a guy who, gee whiz, just wished the team with which he'd recently become associated could win an occasional championship. But after George Bush singled out several nations as "the axis of evil," the majority of people who vote took him seriously, and Bush accumulated what he called "the political capital" that enabled him to benefit the people and corporations that had installed him in the presidency, to further impoverish the least fortunate citizens in his own country, and to set in motion the bombings and invasions that have killed God knows how many people elsewhere as well as Pat Tillman and a couple thousand other Americans.

No game that, and, judging by precedent, no apology anticipated. No time outs, either, and no more games for those who lose, and, heaven help us, apparently no clock.

Notes

1. The most complete account I've found of the story of Pat Tillman's death and its aftermath was written by Steve Coll for the *Washington Post*. The article

subsequently appeared in *Best American Sports Writing 2005*, ed. Mike Lupika (Boston: Houghton Mifflin, 2005), where I saw it. The passage I've quoted appears on page 181 of the article as presented in that collection, and much of the rest of the material relating to Pat Tillman comes from that article as well.

2. Coll, 191.

3. Coll, 196.

4. Wilfred Owen, "Dulce et Decorum Est," 1917. The Latin phrase can be translated as "It is sweet and right to die for your country."

5. I agree with the many people who've suggested that the best way to support the troops is to support policy that won't require them to go to war, and to work to bring home those who have gone to war. It is easier to support soldiers who make the decision to refuse to participate in invasions like the war in Iraq, and my own dream is of a day when so many young people in so many different countries refuse to fight each other for the purpose old men have contrived that the enterprise of war collapses . . . but that's a topic for another day.

Re-Writing History

3/5/2003

I'd like to be in Florida, or out West in the sun,
Where baseball players stretch and toss, and sometimes almost run . . .
Where time stands still beneath blue skies on green and glowing land,
And there is nothing much to think about or understand.

I'd like to be in Arizona or beside the sea,
Where ancient men in sun hats largely let each other be,
And talk, if talk they do, about the new kid out in left,
And listen to the "tock" of batting practice, quite bereft
Of reason for concern, or any worry big or small
That's not within the arc of that bright, painted outfield wall

Outside the bubble of the game as it's being played these days,
We fret about the gutters clogged with sludge, and all the ways
That ice and sleet can wreck our plans, or snow in sudden flurries,
And then, of course, there is another host of gruesome worries . . .
About the war that's coming, never mind the reservations

Of thoughtful souls, compassionates, and lots and lots of nations
That were content in former times to do as they were told,
But in the shadow of these days have all grown oddly bold
Enough to say that war is unpredictable, obscene,
And likely to turn more against us than we've ever seen.

So, me for the outfield bleachers in the breezes of the tropics,
Where bat speed and the mascot are about the only topics
That anyone discusses if they feel compelled to chat . . .
And who would leave a living with six weeks built in like that?
A crazy man, that's who, and that's what leads me to conclude
The country is being led by one plumb nutty cowboy dude.
Consider this blunt truth, kind friends. Old lis'ners, here's the rub:
Our "W," the president, once owned a baseball club.
Had he but held the job, he could be lounging as I talk
Where pitchers pitch and hitters hit and walkers likely walk,
Instead of scaring off old friends and terrifying strangers.
You understand why I wish he still owned the Texas Rangers.

Polo

10/13/2001

Two weeks ago on a windy field near Kensington, New Hampshire, four teams of female polo players gathered to contest the Seacoast Women's Challenge. I, for one, was surprised, though I learned from Jan Frizell, a founding member of the Byfield Polo Club and the coordinator of the tournament, that I shouldn't have been.

"Women have been playing polo since ancient times," Ms. Frizell told me, "specifically in Asia and Mongolia. And women have been playing in the U.S. since the late 1800s. It's the only contact sport that I know of where men and women can play on a team and have equal status. There's a lot of physical contact between riders, between horses, and the women play just as aggressively as the men."

On the gentle slope separated by a rail fence from the vast field where the tournament is in progress, it's a little hard to tell who's being aggressive. There are a lot of quick starts and stops and tight turns, and there's a lot of swinging the mallet and missing.

Most of polo happens a long way from the spectators, some of whom are fortifying themselves against the wind with coffee, some of whom are chatting, and one of whom is wrapped in a blanket, reading Kurt Vonnegut's *Cat's Cradle*.

On this particular day, the winning team is Rachel's Fitness, led by Rachel Williams. She not only rides and sponsors the team with her fitness business, she designed the glittery purple uniforms she and her teammates wear.

At the awards ceremony, she's delighted that the winner's prize is a bracelet. "I'm so glad!" she shrieks. "I've got so many ties with horses on them, and I'm sick of getting men's presents."

Rachel Williams has been playing polo for ten years, though not without interruption.

"Between a smashed leg and a broken arm and a broken thumb, it's been a little uneven," she tells me. "And then you have one horse, and no horse, and too many horses . . ."

"Too many horses?"

"Yeah, you're right," she said. "You can have too many men, but you can never have too many horses."

I had been told that up to 75 percent of any polo player's game is the horse. I asked Rachel Williams about that figure.

"The bottom line is that the horse part of it has to be automatic," she said. "You have to do it without thinking. And then the game is very difficult. You sort of have to like to make a fool of yourself in public, because everybody's watching you, and you're out there on a horse, and you miss a lot.

I mean, you see those guys on TV in big tournaments, and they started when they were three years old, especially the

Argentineans. I think they're born with a stick in their hands, and they come out of the shoot shouting, 'My line!'"

Regarding players from Argentina, Rachel Williams knows whereof she speaks. That could also be said of her acquaintance with players from the rest of the polo-playing world.

"I started playing polo when I was living in Singapore," she tells me. "Mostly I play in Malaysia and Pakistan. That happened because I just kept meeting people from Pakistan who said, 'Come, visit,' and then I met people who played polo, and polo is like a drug. As soon as somebody mentions polo, if you're a player, your eyes glaze over and you say, 'Sure, I'll come.'"

Williams helped organize a woman's tournament in Pakistan last spring, the first ever in that country, but as far as she's concerned it was only part of a trend. She spreads her arms and says polo's getting bigger "everywhere," including New England. This time around the Seacoast Women's Challenge drew players from Canada, and from as far south as Alabama. Players from England have promised to attend next year. But Rachel Williams won't be sitting around waiting for them.

"I'm going back to Pakistan in October," she tells me.

Given what's been going on in that part of the world since September 11th, I can't help but wonder out loud whether Williams had second thoughts about those plans.

"Oh, it's frightening," she acknowledges. "But I'm hoping that it will be an awakening for the United States. I'm hoping that it will make this country look outward. Look at all the American flags on the bumpers of the cars here. I keep threatening to fly my United Nations flag instead of the American flag, because actually it shouldn't be 'God Bless America.' It should be 'God bless the whole world.'"

It may seem like a naïve line . . . "God bless the whole world."

In this time and place, some may find it offensive.

But as a result of unusual good fortune, a remarkable level of energy, a lust for adventure, and her cheerful devotion to a game, Rachel Williams has traveled to and lived in a places many U.S. citizens couldn't find on a map. She has discovered cultures they don't know and spoken languages they have never heard. Understood in that context, "God bless the whole world" may come to seem less childlike, more informed, more hopeful, maybe more desperate.

Among the things that following games can teach us is that people all over the world care about sports. That's among the less significant characteristics that citizens around the globe have in common, certainly, but it's a start. Among the discoveries that follow are that people all over the world care about their children and their families, their friends, their land. People all over the world are terrified when their security proves to be illusory and when those they love are killed. They are terrified when their buildings and their lands are bombed, even when the people responsible are certain that they are dropping the bombs for all the right reasons . . . even when they drop food after they have dropped bombs.

It may seem presumptuous, even ridiculous, to bring thoughts like this into a story about sports. But sports stories, like all stories, have been changed by the tragedy this country suffered on September 11th, and by the fear that has followed the events of that day, and by the decision to address that fear with bombs.

In a land where the toy stores are selling bumper stickers that read, "These colors don't run," it may not be entirely inappropriate for a sports program to air the sentiment, "God bless the whole world."

Good Old Days?

7/21/2004

It may be true that years ago we lived in simpler days,
When athletes who were idolized behaved in better ways,
And we were less inclined to muck about with what they'd do
When off the field or court, or how they screwed up, and with who,
Ah, whom. Still, I recall, some thirty years past, speculation
That basketball's Bill Walton, on the court a huge sensation,
Was in his spare time hiding Patty Hearst beneath his bed,
Or in his car, or in the woods, or somewhere else instead,
And I received a letter from a friend who wrote in jest,
"Why can't he just delight us with the thing that he does best?
Why can't he just play basketball, and stay off the front page?"
Alas, there's nothing funny 'bout the charge that fouls our age . . .
The trial of Kobe Bryant looms as he re-signs to play
For millions and more millions, if he doesn't go away
For up to twenty years or so, should judge and jury feel
That Bryant is a rapist who, despite the sweetest deal
The Lakers could concoct to keep their tarnished star in town,
Should exercise exclusively where grizzled guards peer down
From towers into yards where inmates count not points but time,
In places grim beyond the reach of idiotic rhyme.
It may be it was ever so, and old times were the same,
With players fouling their own nests, then offering the lame
And vapid explanations that the players still concoct,
When their attempts to save their precious images are blocked,
But even if it's so, and current heroes are no worse
Than villain/athletes of the past, I still can't help but nurse
The nagging, bleak suspicion that we live in times as sad
As they can be, because things have veered sharply toward the bad,
When rooting for a team means not just praying it won't fail,
But hoping that its players don't get caught and go to jail.

Thanksgiving, 2003

11/29/2003

We're thankful for the circus catches and the timely hits . . .
We call them back in winter, when the season's done, and it's
A quiet pleasure to recall the grace of summer's days
As rife with baseball's blessings: agile, brilliant double plays,
And fastballs taken deep, and bunts laid gently down the line;
The images of baseball recollected are a fine
And welcome antidote for dreary, frozen times ahead.
So thanks for those, we say, for mem'ry is, I think it's said,
A blessing. And we're blessed as well by games for colder days . . .
By football, hockey, basketball; by quick and clever plays
By athletes whom we care about and teams that we support.
I won't apologize that I am thankful, then, for sport.

But in this time of giving thanks, I also might suggest
My thanks for games as something to divert us from the rest
Of what we see each day: the evidence that as a race
We haven't managed to progress from that depressing place
Where nations and religions must aspire to be the best,
The one God loves the most, the most courageous; and the rest
Must fall in line behind the chosen country or despair
That bombs will fall upon their lands until there's nothing there,
And leaders, ours included, feel compelled to charge to battle,
And preach the noble sacrifice above the saber's rattle.

It's said by some our games are merely substitutes for war.
I wish that it were true, for then the crowd's insistent roar
Would only echo in the Coliseum, on the field,
And only teams would be compelled to fight or else to yield.
If games could work as substitutes, and war could be transcended,
Perhaps the greatest shame we've made could finally be ended,
And bullets would be only fastballs, bombs would be long passes,
And vengeance would be only batters knocked upon their asses.

So, thanks for games we love, for the diversion, and the ways
We find to think of better, brighter, much more peaceful days.

In Defense of Boxing

8/19/2000

Don King and others who make their safe and profitable livings promoting fights that are dangerous, damaging, and nearly always unprofitable for the fighters would have us regard the Ruiz-Holyfield fight as Rocky redux. By the grace and largesse of the boxing establishment, the obscure but determined "Quiet Man" got his title shot.

For the promoters, the result of that fight was splendid. Holyfield, the former champion, regained his title. Ruiz established that he could take a punch and hang in there, at least against a diminished, thirty-seven-year-old champ. The decision was controversial. The scene was set for that happiest of all outcomes, at least as far as the promoters are concerned, a rematch. When Holyfield and Ruiz meet again, it will be billed as the return bout the public demanded, and some fairly considerable number of that public will pay to attend the fight or watch it on pay TV, and Don King will make a profit, even if he has to rewrite the contracts of both contestants and steal their purses to do it.

Years ago, when I first began reading about the near inevitability of brain damage for boxers, I assumed with the naiveté of a child that well before I became an adult, the sport would shrivel and die. The subsequent fates of more boxers—Jerry Quarry, Muhammad Ali, Floyd Patterson, Riddick Bowe, and so on—should have insured that outcome, shouldn't they? But the ugliest game endures, trading on the sick assertion that young men should be encouraged to take a shot at lifting themselves from poverty by beating each other senseless, short-circuiting their own and each others' brains for the entertainment of the public and the enrichment of the promoters.

I've heard lots of arguments in favor of boxing. Only one of them has ever made sense to me. It came from a state policeman whom I met once day at a gym where I'd gone to talk to a trainer. The officer told me that he worked on his boxing and even sparred occasionally because it built his confidence, and made him feel that he'd be less likely to ever draw his gun.

Steroids Again

4/6/2005

The panel was promising. One guy's expertise was based on his having played in the National Football League for twelve years. The second panelist, a reporter, broke the BALCO story for the *San Francisco Chronicle.* The third was a Ph.D. who's been studying how steroids stimulate the parts of a rat's brain associated with aggressive behavior.

In splendidly brief, introductory remarks, the panelists made their points.

The former player maintained that coaches in the National Football League are not pressuring players to enhance their performances through chemistry, because players attempting to do that might hurt their teams by getting caught and suspended.

The journalist pointed out that as a result of the BALCO story and the recent congressional hearings, more people than ever before understand that steroids are illegal, and that obtaining them and using them is likely to land you on page 1.

The doctor discussed the damage steroids do to the liver, kidneys, and various glands, as well as their unpredictable and often nasty effects on the brain.

When they'd all finished, one student asked why Barry Bonds hadn't been called to testify at the recent congressional hearings. Another wondered whether a policy wherein a positive test for steroids meant a lifetime ban might change the behavior of pro athletes. Then, toward the end of the time set aside for questions, a large young man who identified himself as the captain of his high school football team stepped forward and asked, "If somebody who has all this information decides he wants to use steroids anyway, why shouldn't he be able to do it?"

A restatement of the question might be: "If I've decided

that getting bigger and stronger to enhance the possibility that I'll play Division I and earn a pro career is the most important goal in my life, why shouldn't I be able to act on that decision, assume the risks, and take the drugs?"

I didn't think of a response to that question until hours after all the panelists had gone home. But if I'd been quicker, I'd have said to that auditorium full of kids, "Shame on us that we've made a world in which that question isn't funny."

The NCAA in Reverse

8/24/2005

The deliberations and pronouncements of the National Collegiate Athletic Association have long been a source of dark merriment, and this week's verdict was no exception.

Faced with the threat of a lawsuit by Florida State University, the NCAA has decided that the university's use of the nickname "Seminoles" isn't nearly as "hostile and abusive" as the organization had thought it was last week. Presumably, this means the NCAA also conveys its blessing on the pageant wherein a student pretending to be Chief Osceloa rides a horse onto the football field at Florida State games and hurls a burning lance into the turf at the fifty-yard line.

Florida governor Jeb Bush was delighted with the NCAA's decision. "When you make a mistake, it's important to realize it and move on," he said. "They came to the right conclusion . . . the Seminole mascot and the tradition at Florida State, is not offensive to anyone . . ." an assertion that may come as a surprise to the people, including some involved with the American Indian Movement and many members of Seminole bands, who've said they do find the mascot offensive.

An even more ebullient response came from Florida State's President, T. K. Wetherell, the man who had threatened to sue the NCAA. Said President Wetherell, "I'm ready to play football, start school, and have classes begin and all that kind of stuff."

There was no immediate response from the professors who preside over the classes that Mr. Wetherell lumped with "all that kind of stuff," but I'm sure those involved with the football program to which the rest of the university is appended were delighted with the president's support.

Officials at the NCAA have announced a review of the other schools employing mascots they had labeled "hostile and abusive," but the results of that review are bound to be anticlimactic. If the galloping parody with the flaming spear was okayed, the imaginary wild Indian who delights fans of the Fighting Illini probably has nothing to worry about, and the Utah Utes and North Dakota Fighting Sioux can also expect a pass, as long as they can find a couple of Utes and a Sioux or two to say they feel honored rather than embarrassed by the rendering of their history as a cartoon trotted out for the entertainment of a stadium full of football fans . . . some number of whom are always "hostile and abusive," even according to the wobbly, mercurial standards of the NCAA.

Victorious Saints

9/14/2005

The New Orleans Saints are not the first team to be assigned the task of raising the spirits of a group of people battered by calamity. Of their victory over the Carolina Panthers last weekend, I say "Good on 'em." A field goal with three seconds left makes for a rousing conclusion to a football game. The successful kick could have been upstaged only if some Panther had returned the ensuing kickoff for a ninety-seven-yard touchdown . . . preferably a Panther from New Orleans who'd played at Tulane and had pledged his salary to restoring the campus.

Would football fans from New Orleans have been further depressed if the Panthers had beaten the Saints last weekend? I don't think so, but I may be in the minority on that one, just as I was in the minority when the majority maintained that it would be great and righteous if the Yankees won the 2001 World Series after New York suffered through the horror and damage of 9/11, and, likewise, that it was magnificently symbolic that New England won the first Super Bowl following the destruction of the World Trade Center, because the team is called the Patriots.

People get a charge out of games won by the teams they follow. Otherwise, why follow them?

But games are games. To suggest that the Saints—or the Yankees, or the Patriots—have suddenly become, as a result of grim circumstances, America's team, bearers of a spiritual burden, designated demonstrators of indomitable will in the face of adversity, feels at worst like cynical marketing, at best silly. When the Patriots won that Super Bowl back in early 2002, the team's owner, Robert Kraft, said the victory was appropriate because we were all patriots. One especially irreverent acquaintance of mine wondered aloud whether, if the Rams had won the game, we'd all be sheep. Like him, I'm not prepared to surrender the task of defining patriotism to anybody associated with the NFL.

But okay, hooray for the Saints, winners last weekend. If their team's ascent to 2–0—coupled with the considerably more significant, belated bestirring of FEMA and the generosity of the nation's citizens—will make fans from New Orleans feel better, I hope the Saints beat the Giants on Monday night. ... unless, of course, the stock market, situated in Manhattan, plummets to zero between now and then ... in which case, I guess we all root for a tie.

Alfred Anderson and the Truce

11/23/2005

Though Mr. Alfred Anderson will not celebrate the upcoming holiday season, he celebrated his share of them.

Mr. Anderson, who was 109 years old, died on Monday. He was Scotland's oldest man, and a veteran of World War I. And he was a witness to one of history's most encouraging sports events.

On Christmas Eve, 1914, at the age of eighteen, Alfred Anderson was just behind the front lines when an unknown number of other very young men in the uniforms of the United Kingdom and of Germany climbed out of the holes in which they had been living and from which they had been shooting at each other, and temporarily transformed a field of battle into a field of play. They had managed to communicate across the no-man's-land between their trenches that a temporary cessation of combat in favor of soccer would be mutually acceptable.

Like all games, the one played on that Christmas Eve almost ninety-two years ago was ephemeral. But it achieved significance because for the length of time those young men, many of them doomed, played soccer, they could acknowledge that they were not much different from each other. Beyond that, on that evening, nobody on that field killed anybody else.

The Christmas truce of 1914 is also said to have included an exchange of humble gifts between combatants, the illumination of small Christmas trees set on the edges of the trenches, and the singing of carols, first from one side of the battlefield, then from the other . . . first in English, then in German.

According to the newspaper account of his life published in Scotland this week, Alfred Anderson was an admirable as well as a durable fellow. Praised as "dignified and unassuming," he continued to serve his country as an instructor with the army after he was wounded in 1916, and he took command of a detachment of the Homeguard during the Second World War.

Colonel Roddie Riddel, currently the commander of the regiment in which Scotland's oldest man served, commemorated the occasion of Alfred Anderson's death as "a sad moment in history." But his passing comes with a collateral blessing: it gives us a reason to remember that remarkable night upon which, however briefly, the impulse toward brotherhood—represented in part by a game of soccer—prevailed over our inclination to slaughter one another.

Opening Day

3/29/2006

Ty Cobb sat in the corner, his smile a crooked line,
And said, "I scuffed the ball, my friend. I worked to steal a sign . . .
And file my spikes? Of course I did. I'd file 'em these days, too.
You want to win like I did, pal, you do what you can do."
Old Walter Johnson shook his head. He wouldn't go along
With cheating, or with blurring that thin line 'tween right and wrong.
"The game deserves respect," he said, "from all of us who play.
Without the rules, it's chaos." "That's an easy thing to say,"
Roared Cobb, "when you can throw the ball past any human hitter."
(Gee, there he was, a hundred twenty, still Ty Cobb was bitter.)
But Walter wouldn't argue, though he wondered, as he sat
Among the ghosts of baseball's past what Cobb was getting at.

"The players now are different, friend, and it's a different game,"
So said Lou Gehrig, quietly. "All right, but all the same,
The cheating's cheating," Johnson said, "and law is law as well."
And Casey Stengel cocked his head and muttered, "Hard to tell . . .
When fired, which means I had to leave, there wasn't any doubt . . .
But if my guys had juiced I might be still employed, not out
Of baseball, which, without me, what's-his-name who hits so good,
Is certainly a man who, sure as bats are made of wood,
Could be, when summer beats a team to dust, it's hot, he's tired . . .
And if the steroids help, I'd rather them than being fired."
And Mickey Mantle, sleeping, stirred. A faint smile crossed his face.
He mumbled in his slumber, "Yeah, I'll go along with Case."
The laughs that followed faded out when Babe Ruth wandered in,
And sat among the other legends, grinning Babe Ruth's grin.
"Say, Jidge," said Cy Young quietly, if steroids had been there . . ."
And Ruth held up his hand and said, "There's no one left to care.

But I can tell you, boys, and then I've nothing else to else to add.
On Op'ning Day we're talking drugs, not baseball, and that's sad."

Zidane et al.

7/12/2006

If I'm a crouching lineman, hunched on stitched-together knee,
And opposite my broken nose a guy as big as me
Snarls dark and grievous insults, calls my mother by a name
Impossible to mention here, am I, perchance, to blame
If I jump up and knock him down and step upon his head,
And otherwise abuse him 'til the pig is nearly dead?

Or if I am a batter, and I know the dangers when
The pitcher throws behind my head and then throws there again . . .
A guy whose fastball hums at ninety-five would doubtless crack
My vulnerable coconut. I might thereafter lack
My sight, my wits, my balance, and for certain, my career . . .
If I know this guy's trying to hit me, doesn't it appear
That charging toward him with a bat might be a thing that I
Might do if I were frightened that I, otherwise, might die?

Example three: I am a center underneath the net,
And fellows on the other team, each trying hard to get
Position for a rebound push and shove my weary bulk,
And when they're called for fouls, they throw their hands up or
    they sulk,
And when the ref's not looking, shove and kick my tender parts,
And denigrate my heritage, and finally this starts
To make me kind of wonder if the rules are of much use
When we are talking blatant fouls and terrible abuse,
So one day I just lose it, and I cock my elbow back,
And give some guy a shot that turns his brilliant world to black . . .
Is that a blatant outrage, pure and simple? Might there be
Extenuating circumstances leading to a plea
Of mayhem justifiable, bad judgment half-explained
Because the culprit was abused, insulted, clubbed and drained?

The latest episode to join the list I've conjured here
Concerns Zidane, who butted Materazzi, and it's clear
That had he kept his temper, he'd have still been in the game
When France was shooting penalties. It might have been the same
Result, had he been in, but might it also be the case
That with Zidane, the French prevail? So does Zidane lose face?
Or do we understand that, tired, insulted, pulled, and pushed,
Frustrated with the marking, almost terminally bushed,
When butting Materazzi poor Zidane quite simply did,
What anybody might have done then, having flipped his lid.

There is, perhaps, no answer to the riddles posed herein,
Except to say that in the hardest times, the great ones grin,
Nor do they fight. In this respect, the great ones are the same . . .
They channel the abuse to help them beat you at the game.

The Great Bear Run

5/21/1997

Each year in the middle of May, the town where I live holds
an event called the Great Bear Run. The motto of the race is
"everybody's a winner." It's a good motto, even though everybody isn't, which brings up a father's struggle to figure out
how much to coach? How much to cheer? How to convince a
child that doing her best is what matters?

But back to race day. For the most part, it feels sort of like
practice for the Fourth of July. The littlest runners happily
toddle a few yards alongside their moms or dads. Each of
them gets a teddy bear at the finish line, which can be anywhere. The bigger, more serious participants run through
town in 5- or 10-K races past telephone poles festooned with
balloons and cartoon bears. And in endless heats the in-
betweeners—the grade schoolers—run two or four hundred
meters along the street past the pizza eaters and the face-
painters. The kids are supposed to practice for the event in
their gym classes. This accounts for the sardonic phone mes-

sage we got a couple of weeks ago from our seven-year-old daughter's gym teacher.

"Alison had on a very pretty pair of sandals today," he said. "Quite nice for the beach, I should think, but today was gym day, and she couldn't practice for the Great Bear Run in the sandals, cute as they are. Please make sure she wears her sneakers on gym days."

We complied, and Alison was ready for the first-graders' four-hundred-meter run. She ran the whole way, and at the end she got a medal, and some Gatorade, so the Great Bear Run was a great success.

But as we walked back to the car, on a path parallel to the course, a race between some of the bigger kids began. One boy streaked to the front, his stride fluid, serious eyes straight-ahead. Coming toward us on the path, running stride for stride with the boy, was his red-faced father.

"Stretch it out," the father screamed. "Drive! Drive! Put 'em away!"

Everyone else in the heat was running for second, but the leader's father wanted more. The chords in his neck throbbed. "Push it! Push it!" he yelled.

Son and father finished half a hundred meters ahead of the pack. I was embarrassed for the father, and I wondered if Alison was, too, or if she wished I'd run hard alongside her, screaming at her to drive and put 'em away.

"What do you think?" I asked her.

"It was good," she said. "But they only gave stuffed bears to the little kids. I wish we'd gotten them, too."

Boxing Is Different

11/5/2003

Injuries are part of the game . . . all the games. Check the lists of players who won't be available for next weekend's high school, college, and pro football battles because they've torn ligaments, broken bones, or otherwise banged themselves up. The carnage isn't limited to contact sports. Baseball players get blisters and tear their rotator cuffs, and even cross-country runners pull hamstrings.

But no game besides boxing is set up to guarantee that virtually everyone will get hurt badly, and that the dumbest and most desperate and most deluded or least fortunate among the combatants will suffer brain damage from which they cannot recover and which will continue to get worse, even after they have retired.

In a boxing column in the *Boston Globe* on Monday, Ron Borges wrote of forty-one-year-old former heavyweight champion Evander Holyfield that "the difference in his speech is becoming alarming." Holyfield had indicated that although he was hammered in his last two bouts by boxers who couldn't have beaten him a few years earlier, he plans to continue fighting. Holyfield is, as he puts it, "determined to see each setback as an opportunity for a comeback."

That's a laudable perspective almost anywhere but in the ring.

It's easy to see in retrospect that Muhammad Ali, Floyd Patterson, Jerry Quarry, Joe Lewis, Ray Robinson, and hundreds and hundreds of other fighters should have quit before their brains were so badly damaged that they could not walk, talk, and, in some cases, feed themselves. The trainers, managers and fight doctors with whom I've spoken over the years have said that fighters aren't inclined to listen when somebody advises them to retire.

That's not surprising. Most athletes believe they can play another season or two when objective observers have no trouble recognizing in them the signs of decline. In lots of sports, "almost as good as I once was" is good enough, and not especially dangerous.

But a basketball player or a runner—hell, a lawyer or a fry cook—whose speech became markedly less fluent and more difficult to understand would no doubt see a doctor to make sure the deterioration wasn't the result of a stroke. Only in boxing is what has happened to Evander Holyfield regarded not only as business as usual, but no reason for business to be curtailed.

The Return of the Super Stupid

2/4/2004

Super Bowl XXXVIII gave us a terrific half of football: two teams trading scores, and an outcome that was in doubt until the closing seconds of the game.

The production and the aftermath of Super Bowl XXXVIII gave us excess. Some of the excess was obscene, and it had nothing to do with tear-away clothing.

Legal wagering on Sunday's game topped 81 million dollars, a record, and the Nevada sports books won 12.4 million, also a record. Sunday was a wonderful day to be a bookie in Las Vegas.

Nobody can reliably calculate how much was bet illegally on the game, or how many losers will have their legs broken over the next few weeks. Sunday night one guy who'd bet the wrong way jumped off the Bronx-Whitestone bridge in New York. He survived, so he still owes, I guess.

In Boston, an excess of stupidity and violence was evident in the partying that followed the game. Celebrants, spelled i-d-i-o-t-s, overturned cars, set fires, and got arrested. One young man was killed by a drunk driver who plowed his car into a crowd.

Meanwhile a portion of the crowd at the game in Houston set a new standard for cruelty at the Super Bowl . . . maybe for anywhere. When the security guards at one entrance to Reliant Stadium opened a gate to allow early admission to a group of Make-A-Wish Foundation children, impatient fans at an adjacent entrance began howling. One of the guards explained to the crowd that the kids had cancer. Some of them were in wheelchairs.

No doubt the guard wished he hadn't said anything when members of the mob began chanting "cancer kids can't cut." One woman bellowed "bleep the cripples," and the "bleep" was precisely what you think it was. One man yelled, "I'll take the chemo!"

Remarkably, according to the aunt of one of the children, a fifteen-year-old boy in remission from Ewing's Sarcoma, the adults accompanying the Make-A-Wish Foundation children managed to refrain from attacking the chanters. Even more remarkably, according to Make-A-Wish Foundation spokesperson Jim Maggio, the vicious, stupid behavior of a mob of drunken adults didn't spoil the day. Though some of the smaller children were frightened, most of the kids had a wonderful time at the game.

I suppose that last bit constitutes a happy ending. In the context of this insane story, it's the best I can do.

The Honorable Gentlemen?

12/8/2004

Four of our elected leaders have recently weighed in on the issue of steroids in baseball. George Bush came out against in his State of the Union address. Senator John McCain has been obsessed with steroids for months. Representative Nancy Pelosi of California opined on *Meet the Press* the other day that pro ballplayers have "a responsibility to the sport and to the children of America." Senator Bill Frist of Tennessee announced that he was prepared to support aggressive action from the federal government if the steroid issue didn't get addressed at a more local level.

With all due respect, your eminences, what?!

The United States is daily enhancing its reputation around the world as an arrogant bully.

Our troops in Iraq are under constant attack, civilian losses are monstrous, and indications are that Iraqis who want to vote in the elections scheduled there for next month will need armed escorts to get to the polls. The national debt is colossal and growing.

As the scientific community around the world accumulates more evidence of global warming and its catastrophic potential, the most powerful man on the planet continues to dismiss the Kyoto agreement as some other folks shaking hands after discussing a rumor over sushi.

And the president and our congresspeople can't find anything more important to rail against than the fact that Barry Bonds, Gary Sheffield, and Jason Giambi bulked up on steroids?

I'm not in favor of steroids. I hope the folks running the Baseball Players Association will see that coming to some agreement with the commissioner to set up a testing and discipline program similar to the ones in the other pro sports would be good public relations.

Will such a program end the use of banned and dangerous substances by baseball players? No, it won't . . . no more than tougher programs in the NBA and the NFL have ended the use of banned and dangerous substances by basketball and football players.

But nobody except players trying to set records or players and coaches trying to hold on to their jobs is for steroids. So it's a lot easier and less risky for politicians to come out loudly for purity in baseball rather than, say, an honest, sane, and responsible foreign policy, comprehensive, universal health coverage, or a cooperative, international energy plan.

Ah. I get it. Never mind.

Casey in the Twilight Zone

3/9/2005

On Monday in San Diego, at a symposium of the International Society for Optical Engineers on Smart Structures, three robot-arms designed and programmed to arm wrestle a human opponent lost.

Despite "electroactive polymers," which are bendable plastic constructions that can be stimulated to change shape as muscles do, none of the machines could beat a seventeen-year-old girl who characterized herself as "not very strong."

But science sprints and lurches on, and it's not hard to imagine the development of a polymer—or some other muscle-like, throbbing construction—that could be grafted on to the injured portion of a pitcher's arm and then stimulated to competitive ends. And if, after surgery and rehab, that pitcher were throwing eight miles an hour faster than he could before he was injured, would he be allowed to return to the game? What if he still threw his pre-injury fastball, but his arm were less prone to fatigue? And what about a pitcher who's never been injured, but who just decided—perhaps with the enthusiastic, financial encouragement of his employers—to have the bionic arm operation the way some people with perfectly good noses decide they need smaller ones? Would it be okay to have a polymer-enhanced shoulder if you'd shredded the original equipment throwing fast balls, but not okay if you'd opted for proactive surgery?

This may be the next technological/pharmacological leap to drive a commissioner of baseball into self-righteous fits of contradictory harrumphing. The questions accompanying a development like the enhanced arm may be the twenty-first century extension of the questions Bud Selig faces now: where is the line between rehabilitation and the augmentation of one's physical potential via chemical means? Should a professional baseball player be prohibited from ingesting a substance or taking advantage of a procedure available to anybody who isn't a professional baseball player? Should a distinction be made between stimulants and other substances and treatments that are potentially harmful, and those that, as far as anyone has been able to determine, are not?

There was a time when I thought it would be fun to be the commissioner of baseball. But I'm happy that I'm not the commissioner of baseball now, and I'm happier that I will not be the commissioner of baseball in some potentially more juiced-up and complicated future.

Progress

A while back at a New Hampshire Humanities Foundation Symposium entitled "Sport and the American Experience," I found myself in the company of a number of women who are—or have been—extraordinary athletes. From their personal experiences they came up with various perspectives on the status of women in sports today.

Jane Blalock, the winner of twenty-nine tournaments on the LPGA tour through 1985, is a businesswoman now. She told a story of a business appointment she'd had recently at a country club where she is a member. Part way through lunch, a club functionary came to the table and told her she'd have to leave, since women—even businesswomen—weren't allowed in the grille room at that hour.

"I'm sorry," the functionary said.

"Not as sorry as you're gonna be," Ms. Blalock told him.

I'm inclined to believe her.

There were other stories about bad old days more distant. One woman in her fifties remembered that during her years as a high school athlete there were no showers in the girls' locker room.

"I guess the idea was that we weren't supposed to sweat," the woman, still an expert skier, shrugged. "And, God help us, we didn't complain."

A third woman, Lee Delfosse, was a member of the U.S. Ski Team thirty years ago and wins seniors tennis tournaments today, so her athletic triumphs have spanned both eras: the one in which the girls had no showers, and the one in which women can't use the grille room for business lunches.

But in talking about sports to a room full of people, Ms. Delfosse was not only upbeat, she was poetic: "I love the excellence which sports has demanded of me," she said. "I can recreate myself each time I compete."

I'm glad she said that. I wish I'd thought of it myself. It makes me feel as if—regarding the issue of the access that girls and women have to the benefits of sports—we haven't entirely failed, though there is considerable distance to go.

A final story from the Humanities Foundation Symposium goes beyond the matter of gender and illuminates the inclination of our culture—and perhaps our species—to twist the positive potential of an athletic achievement into shame and self-loathing.

The storyteller was Penny Pitou. Today, Ms. Pitou is an entrepreneur. She coordinates and escorts ski trips to Europe and hiking expeditions in the Alps. But thirty-five years ago in Squaw Valley, she became the first American skier to win an Olympic medal in a downhill event. It was a silver medal, and therein hangs a tale. On the very day she won it, she received a visit from the vice president of the United States.

"I was really thrilled," Penny Pitou recalls. "I was in the dormitory, and somebody came running up the hall to tell me that Richard Nixon was in the lobby, asking for me. He shook my hand, and I can remember seeing the little, black hairs on his nose twitching, and he said, 'Miss Pitou, I understand you came in second, I'm sorry.'

"I told him, 'But, Mr. Vice President, I won a silver medal.'

"He said, 'Yes, but don't feel badly. Tomorrow you'll have another opportunity to win a gold medal.'

"I was really depressed for about ten seconds. Then I realized that, of course, I should be proud of myself for winning the silver medal. In my other event I won another silver medal, which was great, and I couldn't help giggling about Vice President Nixon probably brooding over the fact that—as far as he was concerned—I'd failed again."

The happy ending to Penny Pitou's story, then and now, is that she could and can see—and thereby help us see—

through the assumption, equally stern and silly, that unless you finish first, you're a loser. (Sometimes, in fact, those who finish first are the most spectacular losers, but that's probably fodder for another day's commentary.)

The point here—and it was a point that kept surfacing in the context of the discussion of various sports throughout the symposium—is that, properly understood, our games give our children and the rest of us marvelous opportunities. We can learn and re-learn that working hard at something tends to make us better at it, as well as increase our self-respect. Within the comfortable context of rules, we can know the joy of pushing ourselves, and of growing in strength and grace, and perhaps of accomplishing more than we thought we could accomplish.

And if we can only keep our heads on straight when somebody tells us that if we don't finish first, we should be unhappy, much more often than not we'll be better off for having played the game.

Dark Garden

9/17/2004

(The winter of 2004–5 lacked hockey. More specifically, in Boston, that winter lacked the Bruins. There are those who resent that circumstance.)

There's murmuring down Causeway Street of empty winter nights.
They'll lack, I fear, the goals, the checks, and then, of course,
   the fights.
The season, thanks to bickering, has fallen into ruins
Before it's even started. And for those who love the Bruins,
The great, blank months loom dark and bleak. On bitter gall they sup,
For there may be no chase this year for Stanley's shining cup.

What else gives winter meaning? Scraping ice from off your car?
Or getting lost in swirling snow and won'dring where you are?
Or skiing? where you freeze your feet and break your aging bones?

Or how 'bout curling? brushing paths for stupid, sliding stones?
Look, winter here is hockey. It's the game folks here adore.
It's been that way since glory walked among us, Bobby Orr . . .
Nah, "walked among" is not the term. It's flyin's what he did.
And what a falling off is here, now hockey's off the grid.

The players claim the owners aren't as busted as they say.
The owners want the players to agree the teams can't pay
As much as they are paying and still manage to survive . . .
The players say that math is all manipulative jive . . .

Ah, who can stand the back and forth? the posturing? the bull?
The game's the point. The fans who pay the freight are likely full
To well past overflowing with the owners crying poor,
The only solace is, I guess, that right here we've got four
Good hockey teams to watch, although their season's not as long . . .
Northeastern, BC, BU, Harvard, hey, you can't go wrong . . .

Ah, yeah, who do I think I'm foolin'? Winter is in ruins,
If all we have is nights of snow and ice without the Bruins
Colliding with the Penguins and the Rangers and the Ducks—
A mad collage of muckin' in the corners, flying pucks . . .
Alternatives abound, I guess, for killing winter time,
But killing off the game? For now, it seems to me a crime.

Modest Expectations?

7/19/2006

The country that leads the world in accumulating international basketball championships will not win the next one.

That's because it's Yugoslavia, which international basketball's governing body still lists it as the number 2 team in the world . . . though it no longer exists.

When the line-up of competitors for the quadrennial Basketball World Championship that will transpire in Japan beginning next month was established, Serbia and

Montenegro were included. Though now there is no longer a single entity called Serbia and Montenegro, Montenegro having decided to pursue a solo career in basketball among other areas, the two segments of the former Yugoslavia will presumably continue to shoot at the same basket when opening round action pits them against Argentina, France, Venezuela, and Lebanon . . . although the way things are going, who knows about Lebanon? Earlier this week, the members of the team from Lebanon weren't sure when—or if—they'd be able to get out of the country, since the roads and the airport were being bombed.

The coach for Lebanon's team, Paul Coughter, acknowledged that "nobody knows what will happen."

One of the teams tied for the second-most world championships in basketball is the United States, which won the tournament in 1954, 1986, and 1994. For a spectacularly lopsided stretch between 1992 and 2000, the U.S. team won not only the World Championship but also three straight Olympic basketball golds. More recently, the United States has finished sixth and third in international competition.

This week, under the supervision of Duke coach Mike Krzyzewski, Lebron James, Dwyane Wade, and a collection of other NBA players will begin practicing in Las Vegas for the tournament that begins next month.

Already the sporting press in the United States has begun writing things like "anything less than gold will be deemed an unqualified downer."

It's easy to see how reporters, columnists, and others in the United States could view the tournament in those terms. Basketball once was ours. The fall from that height was sudden and precipitous.

On the other hand, given current circumstances, maybe we should view the World Basketball Championships as a success if each of the teams is able to get to Japan, and if none of the rest of the competing nations disintegrates before the medals ceremony. No matter who wins, maybe we should be celebrating the opportunity to play.

What Then Must We Do?

9/18/2001

I don't believe we have a duty to pay attention to the games that have begun again. I don't see attending a ballgame as a patriotic act. The resumption of that particular routine doesn't seem likely to me to discourage terrorists hoping to disrupt the rhythm of the nation.

On the good days, we watch sports for more fundamental reasons, and I think those reasons hold. On Monday morning, a day of perfect September weather, I wandered over to the soccer field where about a dozen members of the Boston Breakers were practicing. The women's pro soccer league season ended almost a month ago. It was not interrupted by last Tuesday's terrifying attacks. But the Breakers will play an exhibition game early next month as part of a ceremony at the Soccer Hall of Fame, so practice was in order.

In a tight square, the Breakers played an intricate game of keep-away that required precise, one-touch passes. They hopped and slid and skidded to stop balls lined across the square and, looking left, redirected balls to the right with their arches, knees, or foreheads. They laughed and cheered each others' good gets and hooted when somebody flubbed a pass.

On this bright day, there were no autograph seekers, no little girls with faces painted blue, no soccer moms or soccer dads. In fact, there was nobody watching the practice but me. The players were performing for nobody but themselves and their coach, who offered some direction without seeming to alter the creative, spontaneous exercise of thumping the ball adroitly to a new place, where it would find a player whose feet knew what to do with it next: back-heel it, step over it with the right foot and dump it with the left, meet it eight inches off the ground and line it past a flat-footed defender.

The Breakers did not seem to be playing because it was their duty to carry on their profession. I don't think they had in mind the confounding of terrorists who aimed to knock a nation off stride. They seemed to be playing for the love of it, and in watching them, I was reminded of why we watch. It is for the temporary connection to beauty that the game offers: the beauty of the perfect move, selected and executed for its own sake; the joy of the marriage of talent and skill developed from hard practice. It's an image that celebrates life as well as any in a time when we need such celebrations, not to discourage madmen, but to delight, reassure, and enrich our shaken selves.